COLLEGE BASICS:

How to Start Right

and Finish Strong

Marvin Lunenfeld

State University of New York
College at Fredonia

Peter Lunenfeld

Semester Press

Printed in the United States of America

Cover design/ book layout: Beth Fabiano and Casey Smith
Illustrations: Casey Smith

If you have any questions or comments concerning this book, please write the authors c/o:

Semester Press
231 Norwood Avenue
Buffalo, N.Y. 14222

Library of Congress Catalogue Card Number: 91-90353

ISBN: 0-9629783-0-2

This book is dedicated to Susan, who brings love.

Table of Contents

I. Classes and Grades

Table of Contents, continued

Table of Contents, continued

II. Social Life

Table of Contents, continued

Table of Contents, continued

WHAT THIS BOOK WILL DO FOR YOU

We give you the benefit of the viewpoints of two authors, one a teacher and the other a top student. Professor Lunenfeld has picked up plenty of ideas about how you can succeed during his years of teaching at half-a-dozen private colleges and public universities. He has tested his strategies with the 4,000 students who have passed through his classroom. There is inside information here on what professors want out of their students.

What will also make this book work for you is that it is more than a teacher's view from the front of the class. Peter is a student, on the other side of the line. He knows that sometimes you have to make end runs to get what you want with a minimum of time and energy.

If the U.S. Army were run like American colleges and universities, there would be no Basic Training. Recruits would be forced to figure it out for themselves. Should they buy rifles? How about boots? After a week of partying with the platoon they would all be shipped off to the front lines. You'd better believe that if the Army did work like that the casualties would be heavy. They sure are in college. *Forty out of a hundred of any year's entering students will never graduate.* The word's not getting out about how to succeed.

Some students arrive at school well prepared. They graduated from elite prep schools and the very best high schools.

Their teachers told them exactly what to do in college. This book will pull everybody even with that competition. It brings together techniques you probably weren't told about, along with solid information you discover only after battling it out, term after term.

Confidence helps you to succeed. It comes easily when you find out exactly what to do and how to do it. Daydreaming during lectures? Read the section *You Can Stay Awake in Class*. Want to stay calm and collected during tests? Review *Mastering Essay Exams*.

There are some students for whom the best grades are barely good enough. For them, we have included *Fast Track* sections to get them the marks they require for the best jobs and the top professional schools.

*   *   *

No one will need all the advice and information in the social sections. It's there when you want it. We look at the way diet, smoking, alcohol, and drugs affect health and classroom work.

Tension with parents sometimes runs high. There is plenty on how to get along with your relatives, and on the special issue of living at home while commuting.

Look over the latest theories on how to overcome loneliness, depression, and the eternal question of dealing with a roommate. You survive and make the grades when your personal life works out.

This book presents only the opinions of the two authors and is not to be taken as the expression of official views of any college or any university system.

I. CLASSES AND GRADES

1. IT'S NOT HIGH SCHOOL

Jumping into the free-for-all of college life takes getting used to. In high school, kids were what they wore, what they listened to, and, most important, who their friends were. If you did what was assigned and repeated what was taught, you got good grades. Marching orders were clear.

It's different in college. A student can disappear for weeks at a time. Some profs barely recognize their students, much less know their names. There are no truant officers. You can party all night, every night.

This isn't going to become a sermon about responsibility, but college students just have to find substitutes for the external controls that used to keep them working — the sooner the better. Replace the old prodding with tutoring, advisement, and career guidance. Deans and RA's will really help out if you approach them. All you have to do is get out and ask.

Kids get the wrong signals in high school: only "dumb" people go for tutoring, only "wimps" drop classes, only "jerks" sit in the front row, and only a "teacher's pet" talks in class. That's way off base when it comes to college life. Students are happier when they jump in and take an active part. Accept the fact that people do fail courses and everyone needs all the help he or she can get. Plenty are forced to interrupt their study for a leave, like it or not. If this happens to you, it won't be the end of the world.

When students solve their academic problems, they feel at home in the college environment. Worries about being unsophisticated fade as you learn to handle academics. Social life improves. There are hundreds and often thousands of people your age with similar goals floating around to provide a pool of new friends.

Be proud of getting admitted to college. Only one of three high schoolers makes it as far as you have. Our book will help you handle whatever comes next. You deserve good grades, a full social life, and a strong start on your career.

PSYCHING UP

"There are three kinds of lies: lies, damned lies, and statistics." That's how Mark Twain put it. Nonetheless, it's a good idea to look at statistics that leave you with positive thoughts.

To start with, almost four out of five students are satisfied, or highly satisfied, with their present college. They think that four out of five of their classmates would agree with their positive vision of life on campus. Over two-thirds find classes engaging, and over three-quarters think that general education courses add to their understanding and enjoyment of other courses. Half of the students believe that the chief benefit of college is its contribution to earning power, but three of five would stay in college even if this were not so. Overall, the picture emerges of a big group happy with what they are doing, and interested in continuing.

This information comes from a Carnegie Institute study of 5,000 undergraduates at 310 colleges and universities.

Twelve Items You Might Not Have, But Should Get

- Typewriter — **Good**: Solid manual portable or electric ($100-$250) with big type. Lots of used ones in typewriter stores. Get a bottle of Liquid Paper and correction tape. **Better:** Electronic with line memory and lift-off erase ($250-$400). Avoid ones that require expensive thermal paper. **Best:** Personal computer with word processing program and a printer, preferably letter quality, not dot matrix ($600-$2,000). Look for used models in newspaper ads. Most programs are easy to learn and nothing to fear.

- Typewriter Stand — To get the darned thing off your desk, where you will need all the space you can get. Learn to touch-type, since this is the single most important mechanical skill you should master for a successful college career.

- Dictionary — **Good:** Pocket size, for quick reference (good no matter how many others you get). **Better:** Desk-sized, thumb-indexed, college edition, such as the *New World College Dictionary*. **Best:** Unabridged, with supplements, such as the *Random House Unabridged*.

- Desk Supplies — Don't buy miniature equipment. Get a full sized stapler, scotch tape in a heavy dispenser (which won't walk away with somebody), a staple remover, a box of large paper clips, a package of carbon paper (for the times when you can't get to a photocopier), and a ruler. A sharp scissors and rubber cement in a bottle becomes a cheap "word processor" combination which will let you cut-and-paste essays and projects by shifting around paragraphs on separate slips of paper to your heart's content; if really pressed for time, photocopy the resulting paste-up.

- File Cabinet — Get one with hanging files to keep endless papers, notebooks, and handouts in one place.

- Desk Lamp — Tall and bright. One with a heavy base is better than the type that clamps on, only to fall down all the time.

- Useful Appliances — **Good:** Hot pot. Keeps you in your room working rather than out looking for a cup of coffee. **Better:** Small refrigerator. Pick one up at the end of the school year when it will be cheap. **Best:** Mini-microwave. No mess, no fuss, but there it is — hot food.

- Steam iron: Women will want their own in emergencies.

- Fun Appliance — A popcorn popper. A quick (and if hot-air popped) low calorie snack. Not to mention cheap.

- Calendar — A very big wall calendar. This is where you list assignment due dates, exams, and deadlines for each month.

- Appointment Board — Get an erasable one with felt pen for hanging on your door for friends' messages.

- Two alarm clocks — At least one non-electric in case of power failure. The day you miss a vital early morning exam you will understand we aren't kidding.

2. YOU ARE NOT ALONE: FACING A WORK OVERLOAD

When the work load starts mounting up, there's something about the college experience that leads to thoughts of joining the Marines or following the Grateful Dead full time.

What should you do if on the first day of classes the professor hands out a huge syllabus? Sometimes there are as many pages on the suggested list as required reading. Throughout the term your prof keeps mentioning other books (or recommends problem sets) that would take a minimum of three hours, on top of regular assignments. Do they really expect students to do this extra work? Probably not, so don't panic. This is just well-meaning professorial overkill.

Too often even the required work is impossible. The whole class starts secretly worrying they will fall far behind if they don't do everything. Forget it. It's simply impossible to do everything perfectly, especially when you are just starting out. The secret is to do a reasonable amount of study *consistently* and not become overwhelmed by the sheer volume.

Yvonne didn't have much of a background to start with, but by her second year she was fairly successful. It certainly wasn't that way her first term. No matter how much she did, she kept losing interest in her work and even stopped eating. She felt isolated because she was living at home, and had few friends around who were going on to college. She had not met any new people. About two weeks before mid-terms someone she met invited her to a doughnut break where, for the first time, she talked to classmates. She realized she was not the only one who hated riding to school every day. No one had done all the reading, and everybody was confused about what the professor was going to ask.

Yvonne was one of many students who don't understand that perfection is as rare in college as anywhere else. Nobody's first draft of a paper is really good. Students often foul up on their first exam. Everybody puts work off, and it is impossible not to feel a little out of it sometimes.

The worst, most tension-filled times of the year are when exams coincide with breaks. Expectations for both the exams and the vacation are too high. Family tensions heighten at the same time academic pressure is on. For people who are very close to their families, this time worsens any guilt they might feel. This adds up to tension so it's no surprise that stress results.

Stress is not an incurable disease — although it sure is infectious. Administrators moan about cuts, coaches fear for their jobs, and professors face crippling writer's cramp. Yet, every year when spring comes around a batch of graduates put on those square hats, professors leave the classroom behind to recharge their batteries, and coaches dream of the coming Fall's homecoming victory. Once you realize that stress is not brought on by supposed weakness and laziness, but is a universal problem, you'll find it easier to deal with.

3. LOOK SERIOUS: WHAT YOUR STUDY AREA CAN DO FOR YOU

Students don't actually master much in classrooms. Most *learning* goes on at a desk. So, find, or set up, a quiet place to do serious work. Beds, sofas, and green grass just won't do. Develop a professional work space with a stripped-down look. Put the pictures of loved ones on the bulletin board or dresser. Shove the Smurfs and that stuffed bear somewhere else. Don't place a stereo, or worse, a TV, on one corner.

Keep course and reference books in a close-by bookshelf. Get a tall, bright, lamp with a solid base. Your serious working area does triple duty: it will be an effective place to think, it will encourage you to keep busy (since it is *so* dull), and it will start the process of convincing others that when you are at your desk you mean business.

Sometimes it's not enough to put together a straight-backed chair and an uncluttered desk. You also need a zone of quiet. Often it is not your fault that you can't focus your attention. There are problem roommates — the one who never goes out because that means leaving his TV behind, or the one whose boyfriend is around more than she is. Renting a typical off-campus student apartment can mean having a heavy metal head-banger in the next room. Younger brothers and sisters can be a pain when you live at home.

Sit down and spell out the situation to roommates or the family.

At a residential college, working out a mutually acceptable schedule with roommates can provoke tensions, but at least it will be an agreement among equals. No matter how loud or obnoxious roommates might be, they are, after all, students. Deep down they know everyone is supposed to study, even if they themselves don't. Draw up a reasonable schedule of quiet hours, discuss it and, if need be, post it in a way that is non-confrontational.

There's no excuse for any roommate to disregard the rights of a conscientious student. The RA's and the residence staff are there to back up your request for reasonable behavior. (See our sections on roommates for positive ideas about working out good relationships.) Students who share quarters in non-campus housing have to do *all* the police work themselves. It's time to act when the music, partying, and other residents or noisy friends are out of control. If you hold the lease, kick the bums out. If the lease is an equal share, don't renew.

The ground rules are different when you live at home. Let your parents see that college is no vacation from work by showing them how thick the books are and how crowded your schedule is. Calmly explain that the high stakes require a new privacy and some quiet for a *limited* period each day. For families living in close quarters this might mean that you will have to be resigned to working outside prime time TV viewing hours. If communication within your family has always been terrible, this is a time to establish something better. (We talk further about this in the sections on parents.)

Making sure that the room is quiet and your desk is clear doesn't always guarantee productivity. Major league procrastinators know that they should never start studying until they straighten out the room, the kitchen is spotless, they make three long and vital calls, the coffee and doughnuts are on the desk, the pencils are sharp, and, oh yes, have to get that laundry in the machine. You can creatively add to this list until it's time for bed.

Relax. Everybody procrastinates when it comes to writing and study. The only secret of getting down to work is to start working. Decide on a schedule with specific times assigned every day to the same courses. When that moment arrives, have the book, a pad, and a pencil, pen, or highlighter already on the desk. Work in blocks of fifty minutes, just like a class. Take a ten-minute break every hour. If anyone calls or drops in during the session say: "Working now, call you later."

After studying hard give yourself an immediate and tangible reward. This can be anything from a pizza with friends, to a movie, to working out, to reading a romance. Return the calls that were put off and visit the friends who dropped in and were sent out so fast. If you did the work you scheduled, stop. Take a real break. Treat yourself well because you earned it.

THE 40-HOUR WEEK PLAN

So, college isn't the "real world." But what if you treated it as seriously as you will treat your first important job? If the president of the college were your boss you would put in a full week's work.

Forty quality hours strikes experts as enough for any student to study, week after week. The beauty of college is that you can stretch your forty hours over seven days and not have to cram it in during an exhausting five-day, 9-5 routine.

Think about how much psychological pressure it takes off your mind when you treat college as a job. Forty hours means no guilt that: "I never do enough" or no need to moan: "Where did the week go?"

Let's break this down:

CREDIT HOURS	**15**
STUDY HOURS	**25**
TOTAL	**40**

Distribute the study hours sensibly. Do your homework 4-1/2 hours a day, Monday through Thursday. Get them in when it's convenient, but get them in. Be as consistent as if you were punching in and out on a time clock. Take Friday night and Saturday for whatever you want, picking up the slack on Sunday with 7 hours of study.

A recent unpublished Carnegie Foundation study of full-time students in four-year colleges found that only 23% were spending more than 16 hours study a week. Get a jump on the competition. Follow this plan and you are guaranteed to do well.

14

4. "WHAT'S YOUR MAJOR?"

"What's your major?" That's the opening line for everything from a casual encounter in the cafeteria to the big off-campus job interview.

A major gives you a "home" in the often anonymous setting of a college or university. You meet with like-minded people and join professional clubs and associations. After a while, you'll make friends and contacts and get to know some professors really well. Majoring encourages a student to explore one area in depth. This interaction is one ideal of higher education: a community of scholars committed to the investigation of a single discipline or profession.

This interpretation is more idealistic than most students get. They hope their major will make them employable. Period. Bosses will look carefully at your major. Certain majors indicate specialized skill and knowledge, meaning employers won't have to provide on-the-job training. Surviving the course work shows staying power.

To get their careers underway, some students jump into a major as early as possible. They want to define themselves and get everyone off their backs, especially parents. The drawback of declaring right away is that it locks you into a "safe" subject before you sample any of the fresh areas college is good at suggesting. Hold off to keep your options open. Point out to your parents that colleges and universities don't push anyone to declare before the specified deadline.

Certain disciplines, however, will insist you start with your major courses right away. Expect this if you are in a school of music or in some highly technical field. Check with your advisor.

Some people don't declare until forced to because they're confused or frightened about committing themselves. There's nothing to be afraid about. Declaring a major doesn't require you immediately to take any courses at all in the discipline. You can change majors as many times as you want (before you get in too deep). Switching involves only a bit of paperwork that infers no judgement on your abilities, ambition, or strength of character.

Making a switch needn't mean settling for less. Fred is doing nicely at the U.S. State Department. He arrived at his university eager to be an engineer, based on his high grades in math and science. His parents left it up to him to make his own decisions. Even though he did pretty well during his first year, the course work in engineering didn't interest him. What did was a class in Russian Literature. After Fred pushed the paperwork through to shift from the engineering school to the liberal arts college, he majored in Russian, won a fellowship, did grad work, and ended up where he is today.

CONQUERING COLLEGE

Now that you are starting college, decide on the level of your commitment. Be honest with yourself, since no one is looking over your shoulder. Select a number from the list below. Write that number down now and then review this at the end of your first term. See if there has been a change for the better or the worse.

1. "Well, I'm here at least, even if I don't know why."
2. "Guess I will have to pay some attention because I can't flunk out."
3. "I plan to take notes about everything that is said in the classroom, but after hours is my own time."
4. "I will do what holds my interest."
5. "I plan to put in some study time on the work that I can't escape."
6. "I intend to get my degree, even if I don't like everything about college."
7. "I plan to miss few classes and do as much of the work as I can."
8. "I intend to discover some new techniques which might assist me as a student."
9. "I will experiment with most of the recommendations from my instructors and this book, using the ones I find work best."
10. "I promise myself I will work hard, experimenting the whole time as I keep finding out what works best for me."

The number I chose at the start of the term _____

The number I chose at the end of the term _____

The **higher** the number you chose, the more likely you are to get the most out of classes. If you were in the middle, see if any sections of this book can help. Selecting a really low number as an honest assessment of your values signals trouble ahead.

Start looking for sympathetic people to help you settle in. Being engaged in college classes will aid you in raising the level of your commitment and make success more of a sure thing.

5. PLAN FOR CHANGE

After the first few semesters, most students come to believe their major fully defines them, and the entire college experience. Yet, courses in the major are only from one-quarter to less than one-third of the credit total.

The major doesn't mean quite as much as advisors tell you. Departments stir up a frenzy of anxiety about what employers are alleged to want, which always comes down to more credits in the major. The reason they plug their own courses is clear: colleges and universities allocate funds to departments by a not-so-subtle "body count."

While you may feel that the major defines you in college, outside college what counts most is that you will have a degree. The major may help you get the first job, but after that employers pay little attention to what your major was, since performance in the workplace takes over as the criterion for promotion or career moves.

By the second job, no one bothers with transcripts, which will probably come as a great relief to you. This means that within a few years of working you will no longer be locked into any pattern set in school. It's a good thing that nobody's long-term career relies on the choice of a major or, worse, on a few grades that weren't so terrific.

Scare talk about "unemployable disciplines" doesn't make much sense, either. If someone wants to major in the liberal and fine arts or another entirely academic area, they should go right ahead. Admittedly, the entry level jobs with the biggest starting salaries usually go to people with technical training.

Government statistics do show, though, that other graduates catch up with, and often surpass, the narrowly technically trained during the mid-career peak earning years. This is because high-level advancement requires conceptual and communication skills. Ours is a very mobile society. Statistics show that in a few years most employees are doing something quite different from that in which they majored. Be aware of this typical after-college job cycle.

While students still have credits to spare, they can prepare themselves for the inevitable changes they will face out in the workplace. Even if you really love your major, think about spreading out your credits. Take a minor or an extra concentration. Expand informally into a couple of related fields. Don't neglect courses that sharpen the mind, improve verbal and writing skills, and add a cultural veneer which will come in handy when least expected.

At a minimum, what students pick up in the way of cultural matters can save them from making serious or silly blunders on the social side of the working world. A broadly based education yields a personality that is difficult to define but, nevertheless, is always noticed.

17

WHY DON'T I ACT ON GOOD ADVICE?

(A Painless Self-Evaluation Quiz)
Check Lines That Apply:

A) APATHY AND INERTIA
- ☐ Ok, I'm lazy. Whatever happens will happen anyway.
- ☐ When I get bored I stop.
- ☐ I think I know it all (even when I don't).
- ☐ Just getting by is good enough. Who cares, anyway?
- ☐ How can I tell what advice is good and what isn't?

B) RELATIONS WITH PEOPLE IN AUTHORITY
- ☐ It's a sign of weakness to ask for help.
- ☐ Everyone will think less of me if I show any sign of ignorance.
- ☐ My parents (or adults) held me back.
- ☐ I never had any guidance from my parents (or adults).
- ☐ Older people make me nervous.
- ☐ People in authority are against me. I distrust anyone who gives me orders.

C) SELF-CONFIDENCE
- ☐ I'm not competitive enough.
- ☐ After the first try at anything new I give up.
- ☐ Success is too much trouble. It would mean standing out from the crowd.
- ☐ Self-investigation is something I avoid. My plans are set by others.
- ☐ I can't stick with anything.

D) GOALS
- ☐ I have never set goals. Why start now?
- ☐ I get by now — why push it?
- ☐ I'd rather have fun than think about long-term goals.
- ☐ Whatever I do, I won't improve.
- ☐ I have so little time that I can't try anything new.

How have any of these attitudes hindered me?

ANALYSIS — Add up the checks:

0 - 5 - In good shape. No problem to put new advice to work.
6 -10 - With some rethinking of attitudes you will soon be on your way.
11-15 - Will take plenty of thought to forge ahead. Start now.
16-20 - Going to take work and effort to clean up your act and your attitude.

See next page for "Some Good Advice to Act On"

SOME GOOD ADVICE TO ACT ON

- Stop "shooting yourself in the foot." Listen carefully; double check dates; don't lose paperwork; and get a good alarm clock.
- Get used to asking for advice. Put your doubts and feelings into words.
- Start setting higher expectations. Stop feeling sorry for yourself.
- Recognize that people in authority are not automatically out to get you.
- Not everyone who appears cold and distant really is. Give them a second chance.
- No one expects you to know anything at first. It's the wiliingness to learn and change that counts.
- Always weigh the value of putting a little time in to learn a new technique against all the extra time wasted by continuing with something that just barely works.
- If something doesn't work out the first time, try it again, later on.
- Keep in mind you have a whole lifetime ahead to have fun and to socialize.
- Remind yourself you really are capable.

6. YOU CAN STAY AWAKE IN CLASS

Across North America teachers drone on while students slump, brain-dead, in their seats. Want proof? When surveyed, over 90% of college students admitted that they had been totally bored in some classes. No surprise. Don't expect lectures to compete with David Letterman's shows or Stephen Spielberg's movies. Some classes will always be more interesting than others due to unusual subject matter or a great teacher. Unfortunately, these few courses will always be the exception, not the rule. Students looking to be entertained won't give each course the full shot. They become disappointed, waste their time doodling or tuning out, and end up with bad grades.

The way to cut through the fog is to become an aggressive learner. It keeps your mind from wandering, even in the dreariest situations. Follow the argument presented by the instructor, even if it is confused. Take notes constantly, no matter how little there is to pick up. During slow patches, set up questions in your notes: "What does this mean?" "What is the significance of this point?" "Where does this idea or fact fit into everything else I have learned?"

Question the prof from time to time to break up the endless droning. Pitch into dull discussions. Students who are fully engaged don't fall asleep with their eyes open. There are also mechanical ways to stay awake. Removing one shoe (but not both) sets up a temperature difference. Take deep breaths to fill your lungs with oxygen.

Drifting off is a strong sign that terminal boredom has been allowed to set in. This is a sure way to get in bad with teachers who couldn't care less that it is their presentation that is causing the problem. If you work a night shift job to keep yourself in college, talk this out at the start of the term. Don't wait until you have made a bad impression. Profs are unforgiving if no explanation is given.

You are stuck in class for fifty minutes, anyway. Instead of barely surviving until the bell, try to pick up some material on the spot, rather than having to do it all just before the exam.

LOOKING INTO THE CRYSTAL BALL

Deciding what it is that you think you want out of life is at least a start in the drive to reach your goals. Try to answer the questions below as honestly and as sincerely as you can manage.

1) DO YOU WANT TO BE FAMOUS?
   If yes, how do you define this fame?
   If no, what do you believe are the drawbacks to fame?

2) DO YOU WANT TO BE GREAT?
   If yes, what does being "great" mean to you?
   If no, what word would you substitute in place of "great"?

3) DO YOU WANT TO BE AT THE TOP IN YOUR CHOSEN JOB OR CAREER?
   If yes, how do you imagine you will get there?
   If no, what might stand in your way?

4) DO YOU WANT TO BE RICH?
   If yes, what would you be willing to do to reach this goal?
   If no, what one thing is likely to stand in your way?

5) IS GRADUATING WITH HONORS YOUR COLLEGE GOAL?
   If yes, what will you have to do to make this a reality?
   If no, what is your reason for staying in college?

6) DO YOU WANT TO BE REMEMBERED FOR HAVING MADE A CONTRIBUTION TO THE WORLD?
   If yes, what will this take on your part?
   If no, why not?

7) NONE OF THESE GOALS FIT, BECAUSE I WANT SOMETHING ELSE OUT OF LIFE
   If so, what?
   Why is this your main goal?

REVIEW

Go back and look over your answers. Just in case you thought we had run out of questions, try these:

   How realistic do your answers seem?
   What will you have to do to make them a reality?
   Is it going to be easy?
   Are any incompatible with others?

21

7. HEAVY AND EXPENSIVE: CONQUERING THE TEXTBOOK

Textbooks are always heavy and generally outrageously expensive. Beyond that, they are dull. It would sure be entertaining if your textbooks read like *Time Magazine*, but they don't. Scholarly experts rarely bother to write in an engaging or vivid journalistic style. The information that they provide in their plodding way is vital, though. This goes double for science and engineering texts, which get revised continually to keep up with the latest data.

money on the books they assign.

When you get the syllabus and decide the course meets your needs, hustle over to the bookstore as soon as you can possibly afford to shop.

If you delay you may miss out, because the managers of campus stores are notorious for underbuying so that they won't be stuck with a surplus. The delay in having to wait for a special order may cause you to fall behind your classmates.

That's not to say that Samuelson's *Economics* gets completely rewritten each time. Publishers turn out new editions to keep sales going. Due to an odd provision in the Federal tax code, they don't make nearly as much money selling old books from the warehouse as from a fresh printing (with the page numbers carefully changed to make it tough for profs to keep using any old editions still floating around). By the way, unless they wrote them, teachers don't make any

Used books, which disappear fast, are always the best deal, but don't buy one that is excessively highlighted or underlined. This will confuse you when you analyze readings in a way we recommend in a later section. Avoid writing anything, even your name, in a new book until you are committed to the course, because it's impossible to return a book for full refund if it's marked up. Write your name on a slip of paper and clip it in as an alternative.

Cheapest way to go is the library, especially for literature courses. Take a look in both the school and the local public libraries. This has a risk. Someone else might request a library book just when you need it most. Some people don't mind playing the odds. We hope you will agree with us that only the most obnoxious sub-humans write in library books.

Even when students can't buy or find the books, all is not lost. Maria never went to the bookstore in the first week of class because it would only have been window shopping. She was forever waiting for some check, but figured out that professors could help with her recurrent problems. Maria always requested that the first books of the term be put on reserve, so that she could consult them until her scholarship money came through.

When other strategies failed, Maria would ask if there were any extra copies available. Publishers send out so many complimentary copies of big selling textbooks that professors often have one around. Sometimes she lucked out and walked away with a personal copy to use until she could afford her own.

8. SKIM, READ, AND REVIEW

Pushing through a thirty-five-page reading assignment in a textbook doesn't have to cause excruciating pain. Just don't expect to understand and memorize everything in one gulp. Instead, think of working in stages: *Skim, Read,* and *Review*.

Let's go over a typical reading assignment for an American Politics class. The prof has been concentrating in class on the "battle in the streets" over the American conduct of the Vietnam War. In this reading assignment you will want to pick up facts about support and opposition on the homefront, and figure out the author's "thesis" (viewpoint). The thesis is not what the reading concerns (American involvement in the war) and not the evidence (dates of homefront demonstrations), but *the way in which the author views the material.*

Skim through the chapter the first time around. Try to get some sense of what this selection is all about. Quickly look over the introduction, any preface, and the table of contents. Next, read the first and last lines of each paragraph. A competent author will choose these locations to develop his or her thesis about domestic opposition and support for American involvement in the war.

Because you are trying to figure out where everything fits in during the skimming portion, don't take notes or highlight. Instead, identify with lightly penciled checkmarks what you think might be important arguments and significant facts. If everything seems confusing the first time around, then don't make any marks at all.

The second go-round — *Read* — is the important one in which you go through the assignment slowly. This is the time to follow-up on the checkmarks by writing comments in the margin, highlighting parts of sentences, or writing your observations into a notebook. Circle unfamiliar words or technical terms. This is where the "active reader" emerges, arguing or agreeing with the author and second-guessing what will show up on the exam. Subheadings in the text make this easy; these can be changed into questions. For example, the subheading *Student Protests* becomes the question: "What caused student protests?"

Conclude with a *Review* that surveys the key points quickly. Ask: "Where does this fit into the rest of the syllabus?" This fast review, if done immediately after finishing the reading stage, fixes the material in your mind.

With a bit of practice, these three steps — *Skim, Read, and Review* — take no more time than the old teeth-gritting style of plowing through unfamiliar material, but yield better results. Still seem too complex? Making believe textbooks are novels guarantees getting bogged down and being unable to keep track of what counts.

10 WAYS TO SPEED UP YOUR READING

1. Don't begin to practice building speed with, say, *War and Peace*. Start with light reading, such as newspapers and magazines. They are written so that when you skim you pick up most of the information.

2. Don't read everything at the same rate. Accustom yourself to move rapidly through easy material. Skim along in a class assignment as if you were looking through an airline time schedule. Keep going until you locate what you want to find, and then slow down.

3. Going very slowly will never clarify a text, since your mind starts wandering ... wandering ... wandering....

4. When you start your assignment, skim it first — do not try to memorize anything at the beginning.

5. D/o n/o/t r/e/a/d o/n/e l/e/t/t/e/r a/t a t/i/m/e.

Break up the   sentences into blocks   to be moved   through in bursts.

Grasp three words   as you move   along the line.

6. Never look back. Never look back. Keep moving forward.

7. Place a finger on a line of type. Force the pace of your reading by moving the finger along, following with your eye as you go. This manual aid is not as slow, or messy, as highlighting or underlining.

8. Try to run   your eye straight down   the middle
     of the page   leaving words to either   side to be
     picked up   with the corners of your   vision.

9. Don't move your lips while you read. This always slows you down. To test if you do this, place a finger lightly over your lips.

10. Never confuse reading with comprehension. Reading is only a mechanical skill which you can improve through constant practice. Comprehension grows, magically, as you increase your speed of reading.

9. "EXCUSE ME, WOULD YOU REPEAT THAT?" — TAKING NOTES

A borrowed notebook can be a shock. Most have page after page of half-finished sentences, blocks of run-on text filled with confusing abbreviations, and silly doodles. A few students go in the opposite direction and get down every word of a lecture.

Harry brought a tape recorder to class for fear he would miss something. Every night he dragged his way through lectures he had already heard, pursuing his obsession of not missing a word. He kept it up through the semester and although he passed his courses, in no way did Harry's modest grades justify savaging his social life.

Educational experts say that students do well in a course even if they only capture *one-quarter* of the lecture material in their notes. How can you know what's important? Watch your professors. When they stop to look down at their notes, pause for emphasis, or write on the board — take it all down. Listen for shifts in voice level and for key phrases: "important," "three points," or "to sum up." Naturally, any time a professor touches on the test, put four stars next to this.

Be courageous. Ask the professor to slow down or speak up. They usually accept feedback. Keep taking notes right to the end of the period because some professors so over-prepare that they panic at the last minute. They make the major point just as everyone is packing up to leave.

Instead of wasting your graphic skills on doodling, set up the pages in a creative visual way. Keep space open for later clarifications by leaving wide margins on both sides of the page. Use stars, squares, arrows, double and triple underlinings to indicate important information. Entitle and date each lecture to keep the sequence straight.

In one literature class there was a student so anxious to keep everything neatly classified he would hold four differently colored pens in between the fingers of his left hand, switching pens furiously with his right. He used black to indicate the teacher's interpretation, blue for his own comments, red for quotations from the texts, and memory fails how he used the green. If this sounds appealing, then more power to you, but it strikes us as slightly crazed.

Taking notes is actually one of the easiest skills to acquire because the pressure is low. No one sees them. No one grades them.

A BRIEF EXERCISE IN RELAXATION

If you are always very tense before exams or interviews — or all the time — you should visit your college's counseling center where they will tell you about a variety of relaxation exercises. However, since you have read this far you probably want to learn something right now. This is an exercise which you can repeat during an exam when the going gets rough.

Find a comfortable chair or sit on the carpet or a cushion. It helps to take off your shoes and close your eyes (of course not until you finish reading this). Tense up your muscles, starting with your jaw. Make a fist. Tighten your calf muscles. Next let them relax.

Now visualize a staircase. Imagine grasping the balustrade and walking up the plush steps. When you reach the top visualize walking into a very pleasant place, such as a forest, a beach, or any area in which you liked to play as a child.

Try to use all of your senses to aid you to bring this scene to life. For example, if you are at the beach feel yourself walking in warm water up to your knees. Feel the water on the lower part of your legs and the sun on the upper part of your body. Taste the salt in the air. Try to hear the sound of the waves as they hit the shore. (To help this visualization you can purchase a tape of wave sounds and play it in the background as you go through this routine.) You can see the blue of the water, the white clouds in the sky, and so on. If you put it all together you might actually think yourself back there, even when real snow is falling outside your room.

At this point start listening to your breathing. It should be deep and even.

Now tense up your muscles again, starting with your jaw and working down to your toes. With your muscles tense, go through the visualization exercise of walking up the stairs to your favorite location.While in the happy scene slowly relax your muscles, one by one, until you are completely calm, as judged by regular deep breathing.

If you are willing to take this exercise one last step, think hard about an upcoming exam or other tense situation you fear. You will notice your muscles at once tighten involuntarily and your breathing again becomes shallow and irregular. By plunging back into your visualizations, while at the same time relaxing your muscles and keeping your breathing regular, you will go a long way towards being able to control panic in any difficult situation. When the actual situation arrives, just go through all the steps you practiced. You will not only feel yourself relaxing, but you will notice your mind clearing.

10. FIGURING OUT WHAT WILL BE ON THE EXAM

Professors think of exams as necessary evils. They don't much like writing them and hate having to grade them. Every exam is not a land mine intended to blow up in your face.

The essay exam causes the greatest anxiety because the mass of material always seems overwhelming. No one is ever quite sure "what the prof wants." What your teacher "wants" is lurking right there in the syllabus. Go down the list, topic by topic, to check how well you understand each major point.

Turn the topic headings in your textbook into big questions and answer them. To get to the heart of the assigned reading, look over the index. Checking the index helps to sort out the tons of names, facts, and dates that show up in so many books, mostly as supporting evidence. It gives you a strong clue to what the author considers important. The more pages an entry has listed in the index, the more you should pay attention to that topic.

Sometimes you will have a disorganized professor who never gives out a syllabus. To figure out what to expect on the exam you'll rely on your scattered class notes and your textbook. Track down a student who previously took the course or try to find an old exam. This kind of instructor sometimes throws in a question from out of left field. Don't panic. Regurgitate whatever he or she said in the first place, supplementing this with something from the reading. Put down as many specifics as you can remember, even if the teacher has been vague all term.

Getting back to well-prepared professors, they will not be too impressed if you only throw back whatever you picked up from reviewing your lecture notes. Professors want to see proof that you were also reading the assigned texts. During your review, memorize the points made by a few major authors and the titles of a couple of important articles or documents. Drop these specific references into the test essay. Quoting impresses professors, because that's what they do in their own professional writing all the time. Imitate them and they will be flattered.

Distinguish between the professor's interpretations and the facts or ideas as-

28

sembled in the lectures to back up these viewpoints. *The best test essay you can write will analyze the reading material as seen through the lens of the professor's interpretations.*

As impressive are essays written by students with the guts to take a stand.

Catch on that you ought to have opinions about *everything*, and be willing to put them down on paper. This courage makes an exam leap out of the pool of bland, repetitive, bluebooks.

See next chapter.

ELIMINATING PRE-TEST ANXIETY: A CHECKLIST

Finding out about the test:
- I know exactly when it will be given.
- I made an office visit **before** the exam to get some personal help.
- Someone asked the instructor what type of questions will be on the test.
- If it is going to be an essay exam, I know exactly the structure the instructor is going to look for.
- I asked my prof if copies of old tests are going to be made available.
  (Many instructors are willing to do this, but few will if you don't ask.)
- I talked with students who have taken this professor before. I can guess approximately what will be on the exam.

The night before the test:
- I plan to limit myself to a light study session.
- No matter what my fellow students say I will not panic.
- I have working pens, a watch, a bluebook (if required), a calculator (if permitted) and any other material specified.
- I plan to get a good night's sleep.
- I will check my alarm clock for a morning exam.

On the day of the test:
- I will eat breakfast.
- I will tell myself I intend to do well on the exam.
- I will bring all the material required.
- I intend to allow myself plenty of time to get there.
- No matter what, I will not cram right before the exam.
- I will not let the less prepared students throw me off and make me anxious.
- Before I get started, I will remember my relaxation techniques.
- I pledge to stay the entire period.

11. FIRST REVIEW, THEN RELAX

The ultimate memorization tool is a "resource sheet." Boil everything down to fit one side of a piece of paper, using the other side only if absolutely necessary. The *smaller* the writing the better. Whatever the professor spent the most time with in class, and to which the books gave the most space, goes on this sheet. List key names, places, definitions, formulae, etc., organized by syllabus topics and chapters. Writing it all out nails the contents into your brain.

Really pour it on two nights before the exam. That makes the night before the exam an easy review, rather than a brutal cram. The morning of the exam put in a quick rereading of the resource sheet to drive its facts into your short-term memory. Don't review *anything* else.

Show up at the exam room with some time to spare, to cut down on the jitters. Don't pay attention to other students. There is always the guy who moans, "Oh, my God! I'm not ready. I'm going to fail!" Another unnerves everyone by questioning strangers about totally obscure material. Then there is the hero who boasts about the forty-seven continuous hours of study he put in. Let's not leave out the woman who spreads her nervousness in radiating waves of bad Karma. Hold off anxiety. If you give in to the general panic, the adrenalin generated will drive information right out of your memory. Bring along some sugar-free gum or candies to chew on to relieve tension. (Sugar will hype you up and you don't need that.)

A few weeks prior to the onslaught of testing choose a quiet moment to visualize going through an exam, from taking the first look at the questions to handing in the completed blue books. Sit in a comfortable chair while doing the exercise. As soon as stress begins to rise, tighten your muscles and take shallow, rapid, breaths. Then start again with the visualization, consciously loosening all your muscles and breathing slowly, while listening to every exhalation. When the magic moment arrives, the real exam will exert much less terror because you have learned to allay the physical symptoms of anxiety, on the spot. During the actual test relax your muscles from time-to-time. Ensure that your breathing is even and deep.

Let's shift over to the open-book examination. Prepare an analysis in advance for each book, listing key themes and important passages. Tape the individual sheets into the appropriate books. Put tabs on the pages of textbooks to mark key passages so that you can get at things rapidly. As you refer to the books during the exam, you should not copy material verbatim, but write summaries in your own words.

We should also say something about a test that's far worse than an open-book exam — the take-home. This really is not an exam at all. It's a series of essays. An ordinary examination is over in an hour or two, but writing a take-home means that you will have to put in far more time. Think of the writing as a cram session on a research paper. Just don't load the exam down with verbatim copying from the reading. Paraphrase, footnote to indicate sources, and check spellings carefully.

See next chapter.

12. MASTERING ESSAY EXAMS

There it is — test and bluebook. Read *all* the instructions and look over every question *twice* before starting. Feel free to go up and quietly ask what a confusing word or sentence means. Professors rarely object to this.

Students are so nervous and rushed they never pay full attention to what they are expected to do. When they get their graded exams back they're shocked to see how much they had misinterpreted. So, before starting to write, figure out what the key words signal.

There are only a few ways of setting up essay questions. Profs fall back on tried and true formulas. The three most common openings are: *critique, analyze,* and *compare and contrast.*

To *critique* a passage or idea does not mean saying something nasty. It means you are asked to make an evaluation of, judgment upon, or comment about the meaning of the subject matter.

To *analyze* is to break the subject down into its component parts. Each must then be subjected to discussion.

A *compare and contrast* question requires that you show how two or more subjects are similar, followed by an analysis of where the subjects are different. This familiar formulation has a built-in danger. Students neglect to point out which is more important — the differences or the similarities.

In high school they may have told you the best way to get rolling was to rewrite the question. Wrong. This wastes time that can be better spent in working out a brief — that means very short — list of key words or facts. Doing an outline forces you to fit what you know to the question and not the other way around.

Being "creative" about the form of an essay is a waste, since what interests professors is content. Provide a direct but brief answer to the question in the first few lines. This gives the grader a clear indication of where the essay will go.

Build the essay point-by-point. Begin each paragraph that will develop a major point with a sentence containing generalities. Then follow with a couple of sentences loaded with specifics to back up that generality. Never take it for granted that the grader will "know what I mean."

Avoid one-sentence paragraphs. Graders take this as evidence that the ideas are not fully thought out. Conversely, don't write huge paragraphs, either. These suggest to the grader that a student is unable to distinguish what is important from what is not.

A simple rule of thumb is that each paragraph should be about four sentences long and each bluebook page should have at least two paragraphs. Leave space between paragraphs to fit in additions during a last minute review. It cuts down on the messy look.

Use every moment of time allocated. Hang in and keep on writing. Write even if it appears to be repetitious, because often the exact formulation the grader is looking for suddenly turns up in your final paragraphs. In any case, long essays *always* make a better impression than very short ones.

Probably the worst thing to do is to get engrossed in one essay and blow all your time. Every question which is left out will get a failing grade, no matter how terrific the monster essay. If time is running out on the last question, then drop in a full-scale outline which may at least get more points than a blank space.

It's perfectly okay to write a conclusion that differs from the introduction. To say in a forthright manner that you changed your mind during the course of writing suggests to the grader that there is an intellect at work.

Avoid discouragement and plow on. General Douglas MacArthur, "the American Caesar" who conquered Japan and then governed it after World War II learned this early and one day taught it to his friend, Charles H. Quinn. In the last moments of their qualifying exams Quinn gave up in disgust, crumpled his papers and threw them into the wastebasket. MacArthur fished them out, signed Quinn's name, and handed in both exams. The wrinkled papers passed and his friend graduated alongside MacArthur.

WE ALMOST FORGOT TO INCLUDE 7 WAYS TO IMPROVE YOUR MEMORY

- Refresh your memory as soon as possible after a classroom learning activity. One hour later is better than five hours, and either is far better than just before an exam.

- Review different subjects in successive hours during study. Similar material causes "interference," which cancels out the hard work.

- Brief review sessions, broken by relaxation, work better than one long cram. Makes you less nasty, too.

- Read just before you go to sleep and review the first thing upon rising.

- When a word causes trouble, look it up in a dictionary. Put in a check mark each time so that you keep track of words which give the most trouble.

- Create a pack of homemade "flash cards." Put a question on one side, with the answer, definition, or formula on the other. Give the cards a quick run through whenever you have some free time. Avoid covering with coffee or catsup.

- Methodical study, *by itself*, is guaranteed to improve the memory.

Amazing!

13. GRADING BY THE POUND: TACKLING THE RESEARCH PAPER

Time for a Pep Talk. The single most valuable skill you can take away from college is knowing how to put words down on paper. Employers assume (hope?) that a college graduate can write. In the vast majority of courses, teachers have no way of finding out about their students except through essays and short answer questions.

Teachers don't expect Shakespeare, but they do insist upon competence. Fortunately, there are proven techniques you can rely upon to make the process of writing less anxiety-ridden. To demonstrate those methods, here comes Susan And Her History Paper. Shades of Harvard Business School's case study approach.

"Aargh! My history paper is due in three hours and I haven't done anything yet."

"Wake up, Susan, wake up. Stop screaming," her roommate begs as Susan slowly realizes that *it was all only a bad dream*.

Susan is a hardworking student, who has made it into her sophomore year at a large mid-western university. She signed up for a Contemporary American History class to fulfill a requirement. Why is she scared? Because she has managed to avoid writing anything longer than a thank-you note. Even her freshman composition teacher assigned her little, because he preferred to talk about literature.

Professor Fern Bearzon's general approach confused Susan, at first. From the way Dr. Bearzon (call me Fern) dressed in jeans, Indian shirts, and ropes of beads she seemed every bit the ex-flower child. Dr. Bearzon down-played exams. For the first few weeks Susan figured history was going to be a snap. Susan changed her mind about breezing through when Dr. Bearzon talked about the paper. Heavy writing lay ahead. Dr. Bearzon started her first of several discussions about the paper by perching on the edge of the desk, dangling one sandal on her toe, and observing that history students who could not formulate a research paper were doomed! The nature of the discipline, she said, is to gather information, analyze it, and draw conclusions. Only those who can put their observations down on paper will succeed.

No matter how relaxed Dr. Bearzon's manner was, she had ironclad standards. Susan conscientiously wrote down that the assignment was 10-15 pages, and due two weeks before the final.

Dr. Bearzon emphasized that she wanted real research and not pages of padding. On the board she listed various dodges she didn't want to see in the paper: (1) very, very wide margins; (2) counting the apparatus, that is, bibliography, title page, and so on, in the total; (3) ending with one line of type on page 10; (4) leaving some page numbers off, hoping she wouldn't notice there were only eight pages. No professor she knew was dumb enough to fall for this.

LOCATING
TOPICS

In high school, teachers had assigned topics so Susan was disconcerted when, instead of concluding by handing out a list, her professor said they could write on anything in the course that interested them. When someone got up the courage for them to start was with the syllabus topics. Next, skim through the books, looking at subject headings to see what was inviting.

Two weeks later, Susan had a short list with huge topics like the structure of the American family, drug usage in the ghetto, human ecology, and social activism in the sixties. In the course of one lecture Dr. Bearzon had spoken favorably of *Unsafe At Any Speed*, a book by Ralph Nader. Susan had heard of him and knew he was connected with consumer and environmental issues. Deciding she might as well tackle something in which her teacher was interested, she put his name at the top of the list.

USING THE
LIBRARY

Where to begin? In the library Susan looked under "U" and found the book. It turned out to be about automobiles. Since she wasn't at all sure what faulty Chevrolet Corvairs might have to do with sociology, she got up the courage to ask the librarian for help. It was a pleasant surprise to discover how much time he was willing to devote specifically to her problem. He told her to look up "Nader" in the author/title catalog and "Automobiles" in the subject catalog. They found over sixty titles under "Nader," but just a couple of duplicate titles under "Automobile Safety." She was ready to go straight into the stacks, until the librarian mentioned articles.

Off in the reference section, he started with the *Guide to Periodical Literature*. In 1965/66 there was only one article; then twenty-three in 1966/67; and thirteen in the 1967/68 volume. The *Book Review Digest* yielded three summaries of reviews of *Unsafe At Any Speed* for 1965 and seven for 1966. The *New York Times Index* followed the same pattern: only one listing under "Traffic, US-Safety" for 1965; a big paragraph under "Nader" for 1966; and one almost as long in the following

year. Obviously, something important must have happened the year after Nader published his book.

Before looking up any of the articles and news stories, Susan decided to start with a biography. Of the several available, she chose *Nader: The People's Lawyer* by R. F. Buckhorn (1972). In the first chapter, she discovered Nader graduated from Princeton and went on to Harvard Law School. He had no great interest in making a pile of money and entered government service, at a minor level. After a friend died in an auto accident, Nader wrote *Unsafe at Any Speed* to expose what he said were safety abuses. No one paid any attention to the book.

The astonishing change in Nader's life came after 1965 when General Motors, the parent company of Chevrolet, got paranoid over comments in the book about their product. Executives hired private detectives to investigate him, and even look into his sexual life. In 1966 a Senate subcommittee brought this corporate harassment to light. Susan realized that this was a classic case of a large institution over-reacting to criticism. While it seemed there might be a paper there, somewhere, she certainly didn't know how to start.

NARROWING
THE TOPIC

The weeks flew past. Since nothing was happening, Susan took up her professor's standing invitation to come to her office. Dr. Bearzon crammed into one small space more green plants than Susan had ever seen in her life. Her professor looked over the original list, rejecting all of them because they were too broad. The Nader proposal, alone, might work out, she thought, if it were divided and subdivided until a manageable fragment emerged.

One strategy to get a manageable topic was to keep asking questions of the

34

Elgin Community College

Bright Choice. Bright Future.

Circulation: (847) 214-7337
circdesk@elgin.edu
Reference: (847) 214-7354
libref@elgin.edu

Customer ID: **********8577

Title: The study skills handbook / Stella Cottrell

ID: 35200001956361
Due: 10-21-14

Title: College basics : how to start right and finish strong / Marvin Lunenfeld, Peter Lunenfeld

ID: 35200000226402
Due: 10-21-14

Total items: 2
9/30/2014 12:36 PM

The semester is almost over! Be sure to return your items and pay all fines by May 14th!

Elgin
Community
College
Renner Learning Resources Center

Circulation: (847) 214-7337
circdesk@elgin.edu
Reference: (847) 214-7354
libref@elgin.edu

Customer ID: **********8577

Title: The study skills handbook / Stella Cottrell

ID: 35200019563361
Due: 10-23-14

Title: College basics : how to start right and
finish strong / Marvin Lunenfeld, Peter
Lunenfeld

ID: 35200000226402
Due: 10-23-14

Total items: 2
9/30/2014 12:36 PM

The semester is almost over! Be sure to return
your items and pay all fines by May 14th!

material until one worth investigating turned up. Naturally, Susan would want to design a simple question that could be answered in the space allotted. The student is better off with a "why," or "how," question, rather than a "what" or "who" question. The "what" or "who" question is hard to shape, because it usually yields nothing more than a pile of facts, without interpretation. Susan might have ended with fifteen pages of biography on Nader. Dr. Bearzon suggested drawing up questions about why General Motors launched its investigation and how it was caught and publicly embarrassed at Senate hearings. Further, why was the case significant?

SCHEDULING
THE WRITING

Susan admitted to being nervous about how much time she would have to put in, since she thought herself a slow writer. Dr. Bearzon gave her practical help by hauling a calendar out and recommending Susan set up a schedule right then and there. Dr. Bearzon thought two weeks were enough to push into the basic research, which meant the end of October. One week to write the first draft, with the following week free to let it stand while working on other classes. This layoff means a fresh view when it comes out of the drawer.

Dr. Bearzon estimated that by mid-November there should be one week's work to revise the handwritten text and to organize the citations (notes on sources). In the final week, type it up, look it over for sense, and copy edit for errors. By then it will be the first week in December. Hand the paper in.

Dr. Bearzon set her due dates before the end of the term so that she could look over and return papers. She recommended that Susan always set this kind of advance date for herself. Even if Susan didn't actually get all her papers finished early, this would still greatly reduce anxiety in exam periods.

TAKING
NOTES

Since the next student scheduled for an office visit didn't show, Dr. Bearzon had time to give Susan some research tips. She pulled over her own file box, filled with lined 3x5 cards. Each card had a heading, a paragraph of comment or a quotation, and a source citation. Her source citation was either the abbreviated title of a book or article, with page number, or the name of the person interviewed, along with the date. There was a separate group of blue cards, which contained the full bibliographical information for source citations summarized on the bottom of the white cards. Dr. Bearzon mentioned that the same technique of placing one key idea or one fully developed fact on each card worked out almost as well on individual pages of a small looseleaf notebook.

Although this sounded like too much trouble to Susan, Dr. Bearzon assured her it was better than working from an undigested mass of information in an already overstuffed spiral notebook. Placing the cards in order will suggest an outline. As the writing proceeds, constant reshuffling provides new ideas for the narrative line.

Her closing piece of advice was about what to put into the notes. Dr. Bearzon felt it was unwise to start the research by copying large chunks. Instead, paraphrase. This means Susan should boil down an author's ideas or research into her own words, as best she could. Then, after having read several background works, anything which struck Susan as particularly well-worded or original should be taken down carefully, with quotation marks.

AVOIDING
PLAGIARISM

Dr. Bearzon emphasized that Susan,

like all students, should become aware of the difference between paraphrasing and plagiarism — passing off another writer's work as one's own. It's never theft if a student indicates, by means of notes or other forms of citation, exactly where the data started out. Be totally accurate in copying down, and then using, facts, names, dates, and figures in the writing. This all gets cited. So long as students don't try to fake out a reader about where the material came from, no sweat. Dr. Bearzon laughed at this point and passed on one of the oldest grad school jokes: If you steal from one source it's plagiarism; from ten it's research; and from 100 it's scholarship.

A bit dizzy from all the well-meaning advice, Susan headed back to the library thinking that if she didn't start immediately on the six-week schedule she would never get going. Ten to fifteen pages!

She assembled a list of seven books, located their call numbers in the card file, and then wandered back to the open stacks until she found the right row. Only three were on the shelf. Susan was *very* disappointed. Someone else was working on Nader. She might have to find a new topic.

As she was checking the books out, anyway, she mentioned her disappointment at not finding the rest. The librarian explained the other books might be on reserve, where anyone could consult them or, if taken out, could be called for and would be back soon. One was on reserve and Susan filled out request forms for the others.

Since she had noticed in the *Guide to Periodical Literature* that many of the articles about Nader came out of *The New Republic* magazine, she photocopied two articles from its 1966 and 1967 bound volumes, and made notations about the others.

She had a good idea by then why her profesor admired Nader. He had become interested, on his own, in automobile design. It was his conclusion that big companies consistently stressed speed and styling at the expense of safety. Worse, they knowingly produced dangerous automobiles. In response to the book, General Motors, the largest industrial corporation in the world, set out to crush him. This Goliath did not know it was running into a David.

THE FIRST DRAFT

When Susan sat down to write the first draft she was positive it would be easy to get started. She had done all her research and had developed a rough mental outline from shuffling her note cards around. Besides, she had respect for Nader's courage and integrity. Try as she might, though, something always got in the way of getting started — an untidy room, a long telephone call, laundry, and reading for other classes.

At a Friday night mixer, after joking about her problem, she got into a serious talk with her residence counselor. He gave the usual "you can do it" speech, but Susan was more interested in what her residence counselor called Automatic Writing. This involves setting an alarm clock for five minutes, during which a person sits and writes. If nothing happens, get up, set the alarm for three minutes and make a promise to write that long and then quit. If need be, do it for only one minute. Write in a series of timed bursts until there is a critical mass of pages, which will then eliminate the need for the clock.

IMPROVING YOUR STYLE

When Susan got eight pages done she felt better. Good enough, in fact, to bring it to a tutor in the campus writing center. One of the staff looked over the sheets and assured Susan she was on the right track, having avoided the major stylistic problems he always ran into, such as slang, mild obscenities, clichés, and a stiff, pseudo-scholarly, voice. She did have a tendency to use exclamation points and double underlining though, which made her paper look overemphatic and a little childish!! He recommended browsing Strunk and White, *The Elements of Style*, or the *Harbrace Handbook* for a few more tips.

His major objection to the paper was that it did not make any point. She should cut down the number of pages on Nader's early life and entirely eliminate the corporate history of General Motors. The most dramatic segment was the Senatorial hearings on automobile safety. Nader won national attention when the president of General Motors apologized to him, in person, for the harassment.

THE THESIS
PARAGRAPH

He asked her which one paragraph best summarized the paper. She offered this:

The question I want to ask at the start is how did the revelation that a company picked on a single man lead to seatbelts? This conflict between General Motors and Ralph Nader offers an example of the interaction between industry and the individual in a democratic society. If not for Ralph Nader and Senators Abraham Ribicoff and Robert Kennedy, we would not be as far as we are. I will show that this is an important part of the general framework of social change in America in the 1960s.

Her writing counselor said that although this was not bad, it needed reshaping. The first sentence, he said, took far too long to get started, became vague, and then ended up too specific. He wont on to say that the third sentence was too crammed with specifics, yet did not fully identify the individuals mentioned or state how they were related to the topic.

He advised her to try again. This is what Susan came up with, which appeared unchanged in the final version:

In the 1966 Senate hearings on automobile safety, the president of General Motors apologized for hiring detectives to investigate and harass Ralph Nader. I hold that this public revelation of a campaign against the author of Unsafe At Any Speed *so incensed public opinion that automobile safety finally became a matter of general concern. This conflict between General Motors and Ralph Nader offers an example of the interaction between industry and the individual in society.*

POLISHING THE
SECOND DRAFT

When writing her second draft Susan keyed in on fully developing ideas from this paragraph in the rest of the paper. One morning, Susan caught Dr. Bearzon on the run to a departmental meeting. Dr. Bearzon was pleased that the paper was moving along. She advised Susan to pay close attention to the form of the bibliography and citations. The bibliography should contain only books actually referred to in the body of the paper. Padding the list of books fools no one. Take a look at Kate L. Turabian's *A Manual for Writers* or her *Student's Guide for Writing College Papers*.

Since Dr. Bearzon was in a hurry, she rattled off a few pet peeves. The simplest presentation, she said, is the best, meaning a staple instead of using slippery plastic binders. Heavy, quality paper, not erasable bond or onionskin, makes the best impression.

Susan headed for the bookstore, bought a pack of good paper and Turabian. She ground out the paper. The final version came to twelve pages, with a one-page bibliography. It placed Nader's crusade for automobile safety within the larger context of the recurrent conflict between the individual and large institutions in a democratic society. She opened the paper dramatically with quotes from the Senatorial hearings. Susan made her points methodically, fleshing them out with details. By the end, she gained the courage to draw her own conclusion about why she regarded Ralph Nader as an authentic American hero.

Susan realized that she had written this paper without agonizing about it alone in her room. She had help: librarians, her professor, her residence counselor, and a writing center staffer. Why not get a final reading from a friend who was an English major with good grades? Her friend handed back the paper penciled in with thoughtful corrections of spelling errors and typos. Susan hated to see the beautiful typing scarred.

On reflection though, she decided retyping would take too long and errors would creep in again. In fact, as she correctly assumed, her professor would be happy to see corrections.

The last thing she did was to provide a title page, making sure that the title and, especially, her professor's name were correctly spelled. She typed the date, and in it went.

Prof. Lunenfeld: What do you think?

Peter: It reads like a biography of a saint.

Prof. Lunenfeld: I'll buy that. Not only do people give Susan the right advice, she follows it.

SEE AND SPELL

Electronic help is on the way with "smart" typewriters that beep at spelling blunders and word processing programs that check grammar. Although not exactly high tech, this chart covers the most troublesome spelling and usage issues. It should save you some embarrassment.

SOME USAGE TIPS —

***

Affect - to influence ("Her influence *affected* the vote.")
Effect - the result ("His blue tie gave just the right *effect* with a grey suit.)

***

All right - fine, satisfactory (not: *Alright*)
A lot - quite a bit (not: *Alot*)
Substitute less vague words.

***

its - a possessive which breaks the general rule that a possessive requires an apostrophe.
it's - contraction of *it is*.

***

than - comparative ("One is bigger *than* the other.")
then - time, place ("They left *then* to go to town.")

there - location, place, moment ("The book is *there*.")
their - a possessive form of *they* ("This is *their* book.")
their - plurality ("The twins want *their* book.")
they're - contraction of *they are* ("*They're* going out tonight.")

***

two - number ("Here are *two* books.")
to - motion, direction, purpose, point approached or reached
        ("Come *to* the house.")
too - in addition, furthermore, more, also ("He was *too* clever for his own good.")

***

weather - climate ("The *weather* tomorrow will be fair.")
whether - regarding a decision ("*Whether* I should go is up to you.")

***

you/you're - avoid in a paper when the intent is to refer to anyone other than the reader. Use *one* instead. ("*One* should always be good.") *One* is a little stiff, but not to worry. Professors will like it.

***

possession - requires an apostrophe. ("This is Henry's book.") If that which possesses ends with an s, either write s' or s's (*Charles'* book or *Charles's* book). Just be consistent all the way through.

***

titles/foreign words - underline all book titles and foreign words. Use quotation marks for titles of articles.

***

and/semicolons - avoid run-on sentences with many ideas hooked together by *and* or *semicolons*. Break down long sentences into several short ones. In general, avoid the semicolon (;) altogether until someone teaches you how to use it.

14. "SAY IT AGAIN, SAM": THE ORAL REPORT

No one stammers, shakes, or feels like fainting when they slip a research paper under a professor's door. So why get upset when delivering virtually the same information in front of your class? The worst option is to skip the session, out of fear. There is just no way that the prof will be forgiving about your absence.

To keep down panic, realize that college classes offer supportive intellectual environments. No one throws tomatoes. Your fellow students don't expect anything at all from your talk. They will be happy if you dodge boring them to death.

Avoid nervousness by writing out your talk beforehand. To get the audience on your side start out with a vivid story, joke, or quotation. Go off to the library. A reference librarian will show you where to find dozens of books such as *Bartlett's Familiar Quotations* or *The Public Speaker's Treasure Chest*. A talk on ethics, business, or education could start out equally well with this quotation from President Theodore Roosevelt: "A man who has never gone to school may steal from a freight car; but if he has a university education he may steal the whole railroad."

Next, state what you will be discussing. People never listen that closely, so just make a few major points (two or three are usually enough). Repeat your major points in your conclusion to draw it all together. Avoid loading down the body of your talk with a ton of facts to support these points, for fear you won't be able to fill the time.

Now that you have gone to all the trouble to write out the talk, leave it at home. Don't take this essay to class. Reading the paper will put everyone to sleep. Instead, bring an *outline* of your key points, written out in large handwriting. Type or photocopy any extended passage you intend to quote. You may prefer to put your outline on index cards. Be sure to number them as to sequence, in case they fall to the floor during the talk. It happens.

Rehearse your report aloud a few times to get a feel for timing and diction. This way you won't zip through to get it over, or take too many long pauses. Tape recording the talk will help you make a conscious effort to smooth your delivery. Even better, force a friend, at gunpoint if necessary, to listen.

The day you deliver your talk get up a little earlier and put on your favorite clothes. You will feel better and gain composure.

When the moment arrives, deliver your report in a strong voice. Plow through until you finish the outline. Don't apologize for your paper before you start. That's like incriminating yourself at a trial. Act like you believe in your presentation. This will go a long way towards convincing everybody else it's not that bad.

Look around the room to maintain eye contact with your audience. Find a few friendly faces and direct your talk towards them. The positive reinforcement will buck you up. No reason to get shaken if some of the other students are talking. Some people just can't shut up.

It takes courage to invite questions as you go along, but this is a way of varying the pace and filling your time. If you can't answer a question you lose nothing by fearlessly saying "I don't know." It's unimportant if no one asks a question. This does not mean that the talk isn't good or that they are not interested.

There is the anecdote about the boy who never said a word until he was six, when he suddenly told his mother there was too much salt in the potatoes. When she asked why, after this long time he had broken his silence, he replied: "Up 'til now everything's been fine."

Slides, photos, handouts, graphs, or charts impress professors and keep people awake. Murphy's Law states that if something can go wrong it will, so avoid being shaken if the AV equipment breaks down. Make the charts big so that they are easy to see. Have enough handouts for the entire class.

Sometimes the presentation will be a joint effort (especially in business classes) for a common grade. This can be a problem if not everybody pulls their weight. Discuss the situation with the professor. If he or she isn't interested in intervening, a conscientious student just has to tough it out and carry an extra load to make sure the grade is high.

Professors don't judge oral reports by an olympian standard. At scholarly conferences their colleagues mumble through dull articles, exceed time limits, and exhaust their overly patient audiences. Teachers rarely encounter anything in the classroom as dreary or tiresome as one of these bad professional talks.

If you still worry about getting through your talk, stick to the old army cliché about presentations: "Tell 'em what you're going to tell 'em; tell 'em; and then tell 'em what you told 'em."

15. PLAYING HARD BALL IN SCIENCE COURSES

Math and science courses have the reputation of being the toughest part of the curriculum. Knowing how teaching in these subjects differs from teaching in other fields helps students cope. In an English or anthropology course, the professor will throw out one or two ideas, kick them around, and invite the class to take part. It's different in technical courses, where students are only expected to take notes. A chemistry or calculus professor picks up the ball at one end of the field and runs to the other, under the rule that no one can tackle him.

What this clever(?) football metaphor means is that math and science lectures, demonstrations, and labs move very rapidly, with little leeway for professors to stop and go back. Since the sequence in the lectures is everything, the way to keep up is to prepare for every session and to attend classes religiously. Compensate for the fast pace of lectures by putting in plenty of review time.

Students are delighted when they pick up the main point of a science lecture. Although this flash of understanding gives immediate satisfaction, it's not enough. All that gets mastered in a single lecture is one path, out of many, through the maze to the goal. In science there is always more than one way to apply the techniques.

Tests provoke anxiety because students only prepare to parrot back what they picked up in class. When they open the exam they may be confronted with something they have never seen before, but will have to handle with techniques they should have discovered. What the professor asks is that you demonstrate your ability to develop alternative approaches to reach a solution. A disciplined application to the homework and problem sets, day-in-and-day-out, gradually shows you how to approach new problems from different angles. This work, which sometimes gets graded, serves double duty as training for exams.

Very often, in the sciences, the lectures don't have much to do with the textbook. Scientists have their own approaches or else the lack of connection just doesn't bother them. Be warned, however, that you may be tested on everything in the text. When an instructor assigns problem sets, even if these are *never* mentioned in class, they may well be tested on. We are sympathetic to the anxiety this will generate when you study, but nothing will be gained by complaining, after the fact, that you were sandbagged. That's how it is in the sciences. You are expected to learn on your own. Peer tutoring may be your salvation, if you can't figure things out.

Expect to review the sequences over and over again. Everybody has to. Try to find connections. Relate the new to the old. The way to keep frustration down is to tackle bite-size readings and not expect to breeze through an entire assignment at one sitting. Formulate and answer questions about the work (and its relationship to the rest of the course). If it doesn't come after a few tries, that's the time to talk it over with other students, the professor, the TA, or a tutor.

Everybody knows that they will have to put in plenty of study time. You will have to put in more than the 40-hour week we feel can be the norm for non-science majors. It's too bad some professors don't make it any easier. Scientists generally have a very clear mental picture of what they are up to, but some only bother to get portions out, which leads to frustration when the students can't see the connections.

Scientists use demonstrations to bolster points. The professor presumes the demonstration is another way of presenting the same ideas as the lecture. You may be misled into thinking that something new is being brought up. To avoid confusion, find the link (which is usually there).

In a lab section attached to a lecture course, this connection may *not* be there at all. For lab courses and practicums, read the preparations over several times, envisioning the way you will run it. This preparatory work cuts down on fumbling and clears time to focus on getting it right.

Walk in anticipating the lab results you hope for, within the framework of the professor's instructions. In the write-up, demonstrate each step clearly and cleanly. If the report isn't clean and concise, your professor won't read it. Points will be lost for wordiness or endless lists of data. Make sure that the conclusion has something specific to say about the *purpose* of the lab. Your grade gets a boost if the report is statistically and mathematically modeled. Generate charts and graphs to show the relationship between the component results.

OVERCOMING PROCRASTINATION — DO IT NOW!

Everybody puts off tasks. No one likes to write college papers. No one enjoys filing documents or paying bills.

- Think positively! You *can* get work done on time.
- Most tasks look monumental at the start. Break up the work in bite-sized pieces. Give each mini-task a numbered priority and work through in the order you assigned.
- List tasks on a calendar or in a notebook. Cross off the work as it is finished. It's nice to see results.
- Set up a working place that doesn't do double duty for entertainment. Keep the desk as clean as possible, to cut the distraction level. Don't answer the telephone during study time.
- Make a schedule. Do the same subject at the same hour every study day.
- Plan to work in fifteen-minute bursts. Feel free to quit if you get anxious. Try it again in a new burst. If the work is going along, move on to the next fifteen minute session. Keep a record of the *actual* amount of time you put in. No point in lying to yourself about this. Graph it out over a week. Inch the line up each week.
- Don't sabotage yourself! Work at the times of day suited to your personal physical cycle. That means early morning for some people and early evening for others. Nobody is alert in the middle of the afternoon or really late at night.
- Discourage yourself from constantly standing up and wandering around. Try looping a belt around the chair and your ankle (or arm). You'll look pretty silly dragging that chair around. Balance a glass full of water on a book on your lap. Stand up on an impulse and the result will be shocking.
- Each time you finish a task give yourself a little reward. You deserve it.

16. IMPROVING MATH SKILLS

If you panic or feel hopelessly out of your depth when faced with a math problem more complicated than loading batteries in a calculator, you suffer from inadequate preparation. It's usually no more than that. You probably didn't take enough math in high school because you were not told you would need more. Two years of study will turn out to be insufficient to get you through one of the "money making" majors.

Look at your need for more math in a positive light. Mastering algebra and geometry can add 25% to your scores in the standardized tests for law or medical school, government, or entry-level business and industry.

Lack of adequate preparation will certainly be a problem if you intend to go into engineering. Scoring high on the math section of the SAT can lead to exaggerated expectations, which you may not match on your college math placement test. If the most recent score indicates that you need remedial work, take all you can get. Anyone who doesn't fully understand fractions, still has trouble finding a common denominator, or can't deal with indeterminates in equations is facing boring, but necessary, drill.

Use most of the summer (if possible) to get in the make-up work. If pre-calculus is what you need, ease into that instead of jumping into calculus. Risk getting out of step with other people in your class year. With enough prep in math you will be the one who hangs on, while others wash out.

Even in remedial classes, teaching sometimes isn't great. Professors may jump around from topic to topic, trying to demonstrate all the alternative ways to arrive at solutions. You, on the other hand, want to find just one reliable way to reach a correct answer. For that, go to your book. Textbooks are always sequential. All follow the same line: background, statement of terms, axioms or theorems, examples, or problem sets to be solved. Once you realize that the format of each chapter is the same, you take away what you need.

First-term students get overanxious early in the 101 level when they see other students acing the course while they struggle with basic concepts. Top students may just be reviewing material they already got down in high school. Many a well-prepared pre-med picks up easy A's in introductory courses. So, avoid assuming that everybody in your class has a "mathematical mind" but you.

The basic way to build your interest level during lectures is to "be there." Follow sequences closely, so as not to miss any important step. Check out the notes later with fellow students, for the same reason. Doing well in math classes is an exercise in keeping psyched up.

Women sometimes have a problem with math that is social, rather than intellectual, in nature. Feminists point out that first-year women often bring the psychological burden of "math anxiety" with them. Girls generally do better in math than boys through grammar school. In high school this changes. Either consciously or unconsciously, women decide to drop out of the race. They are told, subtly or not so subtly, that higher math and science are reserved for men. Besides, there is the folklore that if a girl is too smart she won't have boyfriends. "Girls who wear glasses don't get passes," etc. Women who recognize that they have been conditioned to avoid math will put this unnatural interference in their lives behind them and make a fresh start in college.

Perseverance counts for both women

and men. Doing all the work consistently means more than doing some of it perfectly. John decided, late in his freshman year, to get his B.S. in Computer Science, although he had ample evidence he wasn't particularly gifted in math. He liked some of his courses, but hated others, and ended up with more C's than A's. When it came time for interviews, John convinced recruiters that, despite his grades, he had persevered in a very difficult subject. He landed a job at the systems department of an investment firm and later went on for an M.B.A. at Stanford.

Some people just don't want to get involved in any math at all. Since more and more institutions are installing science requirements, look for classes specifically designed for non-scientists and bumbling mathematicians. These courses can be great, but only if they are really designed to be non-technical. Check through word of mouth that the guts, popularly known as "physics for poets," "rat lab" (experimental psychology), "stars for studs" (astronomy), or "rocks for jocks" (geology) are indeed what you can handle.

THE STUDENT'S BILL OF RIGHTS

- You have the right to get a syllabus, or at least be verbally informed, in advance, of what is going to happen in your courses.
- Your main textbooks should have been ordered by your professors before the term starts.
- Professors must return graded exams, papers, and projects in a reasonable amount of time.
- You have the right to have any grade explained to you.
- Profs should post office hours, and keep them.
- Your advisor should know what you need, or at least be able to send you to someone who does know.
- Administrators must respond promptly to any question or request, especially if it is put in writing.
- You have the right not to be molested, or hassled for sexual favors — especially by your teachers or administrators.
- You do not have to accept any of the above-named abuses, and certainly not any physical abuse, from a roommate.
- Protest discrimination you believe is based on your skin color, racial origins, religion, politics, sex or sexual preference, your age, or anything else unfair.

These are your rights, not only as a student, but also as a human being.

If your rights are violated, fight back by complaining to the people in power.

17. GETTING VALUE FOR TUITION

Nothing like being psyched up and ready to go each term, only to have to walk up to the bursar's window and pay tuition. There's a sinking feeling that you're handing over the keys to a new car you could have bought with all that cash. Truth is, you're buying college at that window, not just paying tuition.

boneheads in the old high school homeroom anymore.

Some people believe teachers are un-approachable. Just because someone is called professor tells you nothing about him or her personally. Most professors like their students, even if they don't say it out loud.

Once students treat college as a con-sumer service they demand value for their money and go after help in locating what they need. The most important resources that students pay for, but hardly use, are the professors. Instructors would be happy (if only asked) to show you how to write an essay, develop a photograph, or set up an introduction to alumni for future professional contacts.

Most students never voluntarily go to a professor's office, and so pass up their best opportunity to get inside information and individually tailored guidance. It's too bad students are afraid of being called teacher's pets. No point worrying when you don't have to deal with the

The Carnegie Foundation asked 5,000 professors what they liked about their work. Over ninety-five percent said it was good personal relations with stu-dents. They'd enjoy more contact with all those anonymous faces lined up in rows in the classroom.

Professors may mention the learning center in the first couple of days of the term and then drop it, making students believe it can't be important. Wrong. A learning center has fantastic resources which cost a ton of money in the outside world. Stanley Kaplan didn't get rich off his Educational Centers by giving away advice on how to pass exams. Totally free advice is just what you get from campus peer tutoring, writing workshops, and stress management groups. With the learning center begging to help, take up the offer.

Asking for help is not a sign of weakness. Privileged people figured out a long time ago that advice from professionals helps. Knowledge is power. F. Scott Fitzgerald wrote: "The rich are different." One thing that makes them different is their approach to the world.

Those who have it made know that to play polo you pay an instructor to teach you to ride. They rely upon consultants, accountants, and lawyers to ease their way through life.

The wealthy pay no attention to the America myth of the do-it-on-your-own hero. In the movies, cowboys grit it out alone when the going gets tough. This might be a great way for a cattle rustler or a gunslinger to live, but it's a terrible strategy for a student.

College is a challenge, but not the kind you expect. Solitary struggle with class work doesn't always count for as much in college as reaching out for help.

Go to the people who know. Pick their brains, learn their solutions, write down their references, copy their procedures, and buy in on their contacts. That's what getting value for a tuition payment means.

THE DATA BANK

Annual U.S. expenditure on all four year colleges and universities: $60,000,000,000

***

Watts of power used by the human brain when engaged in deep thought: 14
Watts required to operate an IBM personal computer: 63.5

***

U.S. students studying Russian: 25,000 (almost all in college)
Russian students studying English: 4,000,000 (at all levels)

***

Lawyers graduated in '83-'84 from American universities: 121,000
Engineers graduated in '83-'84 from Japanese universities: 86,000
Population of Japan, compared with the U.S.: 1/2

***

High school students who scored "double 800s" on their SATs in '82-'83: Four

***

Class of '84 who graduated with honors at Harvard: 75%

***

Applicants for Stanford's Class of '88 (1,611 places)
    who had straight A average: 2,368.

***

Number of college students in America: 12,247,055

***

Endowment of University of Texas (largest in the US): $2,927,200,000

***

First-year graduate physics students in the U.S. who are non-Americans: 42%
Graduate mathematics students in U.S. institutions who are foreign born: 50%

***

18. THROUGH THE BUREAUCRATIC MAZE

Campuses are in competition for bodies right now, so bureaucrats want students to be happy. Keep this in mind. It gives you an advantage when you come face to face with them. College administrators are not like high school principals — whom everyone avoided — so drop old attitudes. Relax when you talk with administrators. This way, you build up a personal relationship so that if you ever need help you won't just be a social security number to them.

What administrators do isn't the least bit interesting *until* a student needs help. Then you'll find a little knowledge about who does what is useful. Let's start with the president. Usually, he or she is busy distributing funds or chasing after donations.

The president keeps track by meeting with vice presidents, provosts, and deans of divisions. Some presidents hold well-publicized bull sessions with students. They also set up appointed committees with student membership. Think about getting on one by the time you are a junior. No matter how big the institution, presidents are supposed to be approachable. Don't bother calling, because you will never make it past the secretaries. A suggestion or complaint is most likely to get a reply if it is put in a letter.

Focus on the deans, who really run colleges hands on, day-to-day. Their staffs deal with the first-year class, oversee the Greeks, run the residence halls, choose the counselors, and monitor athletic and academic progress. Students whom they notice get perks — paying jobs as residence counselors, contacts from being appointed to alumni committees, etc.

Eddie was one of the first students out of his room at 9:30 A.M. for a fire drill. He met an older woman who asked him what he thought about drills. He shrugged his shoulders, said nobody liked them, but he could see that they were necessary. She said his attitude was mature and refreshing after all the moaning she was used to as dean of Residential Life. Six months later, when he applied for a spot as student representative on an official committee, she put in a good word for him.

It helps when the people who grant awards know you. The college catalogue lists awards to be given out each year and you are probably eligible for at least one. Get an appointment with a dean and find out what it takes to get nominated. Relax about grades. Our experience from serving on award committees is that being known and liked will often be enough to make you a strong contender, even if your grades aren't superb. You may not get the award, but the effort will gain you the benefit of the doubt when you need help.

Most of the time students aren't dealing with a top-level administrator, though, since they are just trying to get some office worker to hand over a receipt, sign a form, or correct a computer error. Clerks are generally overworked, in the ugliest offices on campus, and always underpaid. Because they have heard it all before they may not have great sympathy for a sad story, especially if a student comes in at a busy time. Try early in the morning, right after their first cup of coffee. When simple courtesy doesn't move the clerical staff, bring professors or parents into play. Have an ally call the staff person and relay your request, along with a time limit for a response. This always gets results.

Be tough and persistent. Bursars *do*

assess too many finance charges. The registrar's computers *do* spew out errors. When you go in to fight bring along every document you have. Standing up to clerks and even top brass never makes a situation worse. Ask your parents for help, if possible. Any parent who takes on clerks, their supervisor, and, if necessary, the division head, will *always* get results.

If you are a student at a state school, there's nothing like notes on official stationery from state legislators or members of Congress. It's not necessary to know legislators personally to get help. Just be from their district. Find out who they are and call their offices. Politicians always have at least one person hired to write the kind of letter you need. It's no effort for them, but it sure works.

MAKE THE DEPARTMENTAL SECRETARY AN ALLY

The people who *really* know what goes on in departments are secretaries. They serve different chairpersons and have seen instructors come and go. Over the years, they have heard many complaints about difficult professors. They remember everything, and with a little prompting will tell all.

Secretaries know the bureaucratic fine points that make all the difference to you. No one else is as aware of the forms that have to be filed, where the papers go, and the deadlines. Be pleasant and courteous. Never treat them like servants, unless you want real trouble.

They will sometimes provide an amazing amount of help. Here's an example. Julie was right behind a student who had just been shut out of an economics course. He was in a rage and took out his frustration on the secretary. After the young man left Julie was sympathetic about the incredible rudeness some people display. When Julie explained that she had come to enroll in that very same class, the secretary laughed and told her how she might approach the professor.

No guarantee the same will happen to you, but make a note on your calendar that National Secretary's Week is the third week in April. Flowers or candy never hurt.

19. WHAT ACADEMIC ADVISORS SHOULD TELL YOU

Inadequate advising is more common than students think. Teachers don't get rewarded for this work, which they do not always love. Besides, the average advisor can't be fully trusted to know or care about the complexities of the entire college curriculum.

Academia is like medicine. Get a second opinion. Double check requirements with chairpersons or departmental secretaries. In the larger departments, however, chairpersons will not want you anywhere near them during registration. Check the situation out with the secretary before plowing ahead. Keep a file folder with transcripts and forms. Hang on to the first catalog you received, since what is listed in there is a kind of "contract" that governs your stay, no matter what changes administrators come up with in later years.

If the program you want to follow is even slightly different from the norm, be sure that your advisor or the chairperson signs or initials the forms before you walk out of the room. This will turn out to be important somewhere along the road.

Transfer students have to keep after administrators to make sure nothing gets lost or misplaced. Find out which courses transfers are freed from retaking.

See advisors *early* during the time period set aside for course selection. They will be fresh and not yet bored. There is always a pile-up on the very last day, when everybody is frantic and the advisor is forced to give less time to each person sitting on the floor in the hall. Bring along a tentative program. That way you won't have to rely upon an advisor's psychic powers. If you have some idea of what you want, you will probably get what you need.

Competent advisors know the killer courses which are designed to weed out students with professional ambitions. The most infamous of all is organic chemistry, which devastates thousands of pre-meds each year. "The course of broken dreams," is the way Fredrick Brutcher of the University of Pennsylvania's Chemistry Department describes it. "In my humble opinion it's used more as a screening course — that's all."

Here is a list which identifies more. When it comes to calculus, avoid the tough one for majors by taking the easier survey, which is for the masses. Watch out for introductory physics, chemistry, and math courses associated with pre-med and engineering sequences.

Other fields have their killers as well, such as junior studio for architecture, or accounting and statistics in the economics and business curricula. Computer science students stumble over assembly language.

Anyone who must take the killers should know exactly what they're getting into and so lighten the rest of the load accordingly. Take the Big One in the summer. Consider auditing it first, then taking it for real the following year. To do this effectively the student must do *all* the work the first time round, despite the lack of a spur of an immediate grade.

All these courses are designed to restrict the number of students going on to the big money jobs. Individuals who don't have such ambitions should stay away from these courses. Ask advisors for less anxiety-provoking alternatives that fulfill the requirements.

20. CARE AND FEEDING OF PROFESSORS

Students who visit their professors at the start of a term to find out about the requirements, or to talk about the course, have a head start on every other member of the class. This could be the beginning of a personal relationship. It's hardly surprising that professors will give better grades to people they know. It just makes sense in human terms.

Worrying about "brown nosing" should be left on the shelf next to your high school yearbook. Treat instructors as if they were coaches, available during office time to sharpen skills, one-on-one. If you spread out a few visits over a term, no professor will get annoyed, and you'll start getting the benefit of the doubt. First time around, drop in during posted office hours to introduce yourself. When exams or papers loom, make an appointment to get help. Dream up a question about subject matter, but avoid talk about grading policy, or, especially, that loathsome: "What's going to be on the test?" It's amazing how much you can learn during casual office tutoring about what's actually going to be on an exam, if you don't put it that bluntly.

Getting to know profs means understanding what they *really* want from students. The class, as a whole, will never find this out because the professor won't tell them. Shocking? No. Unfortunately, it's just so obvious to college teachers what constitutes good performance that they wouldn't know where to start to share this information. Besides, they don't have the time to get this information out and still cover the subject fully.

Here's the lowdown. Profs expect students to be prepared, to be engaged, and to appear to be interested. Transparent lies, missed deadlines, and sloppy work won't cut it. Show respect for the subject matter and for the prof, even if you don't feel it.

Here's an example of how having some personal insight into a professor's mind helps.

In Jack's Eastern Cultures survey, Dr. Shin assigned a midterm paper on oriental religions. Jack chose mystical Zen Buddhism as his topic. He came upon a quotation from the *Heart Sutra*: "Form is emptiness/emptiness is form." Seeing a quick, and witty, way out of a five-page paper, Jack neatly typed the quote on the first page, inserted four blank sheets, put on a cover page, and handed it in. Dr. Shin hit the ceiling, growling he had never been so insulted in his life. Jack hastily knocked out a heavily footnoted paper of the proper length and salvaged some of his standing. That first ploy might not have been taken so badly if Jack had made the slightest friendly contact first. He took too much for granted.

Students arrive at college assuming it's up to the professor to lay it all out for them in class, just the same as it had been in high school. College teachers won't do that. They prefer to demonstrate methods of working so that students will be able to deal with the subject matter themselves.

Joan, a beginning instructor in English, had an astonishingly high level of expectation for her general survey. She fumed because none of them had made an effort to deal with a difficult experimental story by John Barth, a very complex modernist fiction writer. She treated their indifference as a condemnation of her whole new scholarly career and promptly assigned another story by the same author. The sharpest students would not be those who will just say that they "like it" next time around (so that they won't get yet another of his stories), but the ones who will throw themselves in and struggle to see what Joan finds to admire.

Joan's kind of stubbornness is lousy teaching, but all professors expect students to grapple with difficult material and develop new attitudes. Involvement with the work becomes the key, rather than passive absorption of lectures and fulfilling minimum requirements. Many college students find this high level of expectation extremely unjust. Why should they be graded on such intangible matters as involvement, cooperation, creativity, and ambition within the discipline? They express anger when they don't get terrific grades after they showed up every class, "did all the work," and caused no trouble. Sorry. That is the way it is!

Professors are just like the rest of humanity — they don't always put their deepest expectations on the table. This doesn't mean that you can't learn how to favorably influence these subjective evaluations professors constantly make. Where you sit in class is significant. Hanging out in the back row was fun in high school, but you are better off sitting as close to the front and center as possible. Unless proven otherwise, profs always assume students who grab those back rows are dopes. In a professor's view, when students sit unresponsively with blank looks and never take notes, it's almost impossible to respect them. So, look alive and keep your pen moving. Combine this appearance of alertness with a friendly office visit or two and you come out ahead in your instructor's estimation. The amazing part is that none of this involves any brain-bending work.

See next chapter.

"IS THERE A DOCTOR IN THE HOUSE?"

Colleges and universities teach so many things that there are all sorts of folks wandering around campus with strings of initials attached to their names: Ph.D, M.A., M.S., D.D.S., M.D., S.J., etc. The only time this matters to you is when you have to address them in class. What should you call them? The reason we bring this up is because academia is the last place in America where people take great stock in titles.

Any non-medical teacher who has a Ph.D. (Doctor of Philosophy), J.D. (Juris Doctor), Ed.D. (Doctor of Education), is properly called "doctor." (You are not likely to find many Ph.D's in the fine arts, in creative writing, or in fast-growing fields such as business.) Use "professor" for everybody else, unless a teacher makes a special point to be called Mr., Mrs., Ms, or even a first name.

Like oil, professors come in different grades: professor (full), associate professor, and assistant professor. Instructors (the lowest full-time rank), assistant professors, and "adjunct" professors (part-timers) usually do not have the guarantee of lifetime employment called tenure which the top ranks have. A letter of recommendation from a tenured professor always carries the most weight.

If you are at a big institution, you are probably not going to see a tenured professor in most of your classes the first two years. Undergrads in huge schools encounter endless numbers of teaching assistants, better known as TA's. These harassed graduate students lead discussion sections, grade papers and exams, and sometimes teach as a privilege of their "fellowship," which is what a scholarship for merit is called in graduate school. Follow their lead on what to call them, which will usually be their first name. If a TA makes a big deal about the formalities it can be a warning sign you are either dealing with a large ego or with an insecure person. Shop around for another TA.

All the grad students and professors report to the chairperson (or department head). He or she is just a professor selected by the rest of the department or nominated by the administration. In exchange for accepting the responsibility, this professor teaches fewer classes and may get extra salary for all the hassle. Get to visit your chairperson even before you declare a major, because he or she probably has far more information on hand than the advisor to which you were assigned.

21. PROFESSORS WE HAVE KNOWN

Campus leader types have opinions about everything, particularly teachers. Of course, any individual may be biased one way or another but you can usually trust a majority opinion. If you are lucky enough to be in a school where printed evaluations of professors and courses are made available, stay with that.

Even with the help of someone who has been through the system, or a course guide book, it's easier to tell who to take than who to pass up. Watch out for any teacher hard to contact after the grades are in. Avoid the senior professor about to retire and the visiting professor there for the semester.

Nobody thinks about this on the first day, but when the end of the term rolls around and your paper is late, an incomplete has to be made up, or the grade is wrong on the transcript, their unavailability will be a catastrophe. That instructor might be working thousands of miles away at a home institution, or unreachable on a long retirement vacation. Also, you won't have any chance of build-

ing a solid sequence of courses with them in the semesters to follow. Long-standing relationships lead to the best letters of reference.

Some people would argue that it is a mistake to pass up contact with a great and famous mind, especially because visiting profs are usually tops in their field. In practical terms, Dr. Famous is a risky bet for a student whose GPA isn't all it should be. Visitors are unfamiliar with local student capabilities and needs. Their standards could be exceptionally high, and they may grade harshly.

This is not to say that all profs who are around year in and year out are always a better bet. Some of the more laid back regulars run their classes like encounter groups. They sit on the desk in blue jeans, surrounded by a circle of faces and shoot the bull. This buddy-buddy, "think of me as a friend," approach is dangerous. Lack of a business-like attitude ends up in confusion. Papers and exams get handed back late, if at all, leading to a basic dilemma: "What does this prof grade me on —

my well-adjusted personality, my contribution to meandering dialogues, or my written work?"

At the last minute this personality type can surprise the class with unexpectedly high standards and a tough final. Why? Because it reassures them that they are still professionals. So keep reading, prepare for exams, and write the papers.

At least these professors have an approach which is liberating for some students. Far worse is the professor who looks totally conventional, but really does not like teaching. While they may be pleasant in person they have no enthusiasm left for the college, their subjects, or their students. Gardening, real estate, or the stock market is what really interests them. They don't want trouble so they never fail anyone and hand out high grades. Sounds good, but their courses are demoralizing. Freely cutting their classes spills over into other courses — too many lazy professors lead students to question whether to stay in college at all.

A growing problem is the increasing number of foreign professors and TAs with a poor grasp of the language. Nobody tells prospective freshmen they will encounter instructors who speak only seven words of English. If you have been stuck with an instructor who is incomprehensible, protest right away — preferably with others in the class — to the chairperson and the dean. At a minimum, your instructor should be forced to supplement lectures with handouts whose language has been corrected. If nothing improves, get out as fast as possible because it will only get worse when you are faced with preparing for exams.

The profs we hate the most when we run into them in class, or in the faculty lounge, are the sardonic ones. At least the faculty has had years of experience dealing with these folks. Unfortunately, too many students tie their self-esteem into pleasing teachers, so the biting remarks these sharp-tongued profs throw out are devastating. There are only two ways to deal with bullies. If possible, drop the class. If not, keep down and don't say a word more than is absolutely necessary. Avoid office visits and don't lodge a complaint with the administration until after your grade is in.

A professor who *constantly* makes blatant or derogatory comments about women or minorities and tells racist or anti-feminist jokes is guaranteed to be violating your institution's by-laws. Don't think that it will be painless for you to bring charges under these statutes. Find an ally in the faculty or bureaucracy first. Get them to help draw up, and then support, the complaint.

This type of prof is, fortunately, rare. Most of the time you are going to be making choices among average garden-variety instructors. Don't be scared off from a demanding prof if he or she has a reputation for being fair. Amazingly enough, you will get far more out of a course with a demanding, but fair, teacher than you will with a negligent or lazy instructor.

DOCTOR JEKYLL AND PROFESSOR HYDE

If professors are so smart, how come no one wants their autographs? Hollywood evades this question by getting teachers out of the classroom and into something — anything -- other than tweeds. Here's a list of films with professors you'll only find on the screen.

- *The Nutty Professor*. A Jerry Lewis classic, made when he was still a comedian and not a telethoner. At first he's wacky Jerry with an advanced degree, but then he discovers a potion that turns him into a tough and suave ladies' man. This film may be a sly parody on Lewis' debonair ex-partner, Dean Martin.

- *Altered States*. William Hurt is a scientist who uses the university's isolation tanks, (along with some wild drugs) to devolve into one of Man's ancestors. He ends up wandering around in what looks like Nevada, wearing a hairy pelt. Pretty spacey.

- *Doctor Detroit*. Dan Aykroyd plays an English prof who ends up masquerading as a big time pimp to protect a group of wayward working girls. Just as unfunny as it sounds.

- *So Fine*. Yet another English professor — this time in the rag trade. Ryan O'Neal invents jeans with clear plastic panels in the rump and ends up saving his father's business. Sergio Valente's kind of comedy.

- *Ghostbusters*. Bill Murray, Dan Aykroyd, and Harold Ramis were the most popular academics in America in the summer of '84. These parapsychologists prove that they're not afraid of ghosts. Where, exactly, do you go to major in this subject?

- *The Eiger Sanction*. Clint Eastwood is an art historian who can afford to buy Old Masters because he secretly works as an assassin for a quasi-CIA group run by a bedridden albino.

- *Raiders of the Lost Ark, Indiana Jones and The Temple of Doom*, and *The Last Crusade*. Harrison Ford plays the toughest archeologist who ever lived. Why wear tweed, when a leather jacket and fedora look so good?

22. DEALING WITH THE RESULTS

The hardest part of the grading system is that awful moment when your professor hands back what was once a beautifully clean piece of work. It returns crumpled and bleeding. No, that's not blood. It's red ink. Too many students can't stand to see the carnage. They sneak a glance at the grade and then hide the whole thing in their notebook, or chuck it into the wastebasket.

Don't mutely accept marks as they arrive through the term and then quietly settle for whatever final grade the registrar posts. Instead, look upon writing, testing, and grading as a "feedback loop": (1) You hand in a project (exam, paper, lab report); (2) The professor grades it and may write comments; (3) You analyze why the professor gave it the grade; and (4) You act on the analysis by making improvements in your next project. Then you get back on the loop all over again. Second time around, your grade automatically goes up because you begin to understand what the prof wants.

That's why it's important to read over what the professor has to say, no matter how painful. One way to ease the shock is to keep in mind that no grade ever measures real intelligence and certainly cannot evaluate your personal worth.

Tough as it is to go through a careful review, there may be a prize in the box. Professors sometimes calculate points incorrectly and have been known to miss things in their late night haste to get through a pile of papers. Be cautious about how you ask for a grade change.

Professors hate grading because they find it the least rewarding part of their job. After looking over piles of students' work, the last things they want to hear about are grades or GPAs. Don't barge into an office to complain loudly that your professor got it wrong. That hardly ever works.

Whining is not the way to win a professor's heart. Still, if you think you really can convince your prof to change your grade — go for it. Early on in the term, just as important as the grade is understanding where you messed up. Drop in during your teacher's office hours, exam or paper in hand to ask the *right* question — "How can I improve my work in your class?" Even a student ecstatic to see an A on a quiz or paper should follow-up (especially if there are few written comments), so as to maintain this high performance. Find out what the secret was, because professors typically, and unfortunately, give high achievers less advice than they do floundering students.

Teachers are willing to talk at greater length about research papers than exams. A project has much more to do with every professors' interests and methods of working than does any kind of exam. This is why teachers encourage rewrites. If there is enough time left in the semester, you should take them up on it and revise your papers. Do this only when the ground rules are clear and when the rewrites will not get in the way of your other work.

See next chapter.

58

FOLLOW-UP: HOW MANY STUDY TIPS
HAVE I PUT INTO ACTION?

Fill in the points for each category:

a) CHOOSE TO SIT:
_____ at the front or middle of room (2 points)
_____ along the far sides (1 point)
_____ in the back (0 points)

b) DO MY ASSIGNMENTS BEFORE ATTENDING LECTURES:
_____ usually (3 points)
_____ occasionally (1 point)
_____ rarely (0 points)

c) ATTEMPT TO TAKE CLEAR NOTES IN CLASS:
_____ usually (3 points)
_____ sometimes (2 points)
_____ rarely (0 points)

d) ASK QUESTIONS IN CLASS:
_____ usually (3 points)
_____ sometimes (2 points)
_____ never (0 points)

e) TAKE PART IN DISCUSSIONS:
_____ usually (3 points)
_____ sometimes (2 points)
_____ never (0 points)

f) NUMBER OF UNEXCUSED ABSENCES THUS FAR:
_____ none (5 points)
_____ under all allowed maximums (3 points)
_____ over any allowed maximum (0 points)

g) DECIDED TO VISIT AT LEAST ONE PROFESSOR IN HIS/HER OFFICE:
_____ yes (1 point)
_____ no (0 points)

h) TALKED WITH AN ADMINISTRATOR WHEN IT WASN'T REQUIRED:
_____ yes (1 point)
_____ no (0 points)

(continued next page)

Study Tips into Action, continued

i) STUDY FOR MY EXAMS:
_____ a week ahead or over breaks (3 points)
_____ two nights before (2 points)
_____ night before (0 points)

j) PRACTICED A RELAXATION TECHNIQUE BEFORE AN EXAM
 OR ORAL PRESENTATION:
_____ tried it (1 point)
_____ never (0 points)

k) DURING EXAMS, I:
_____ took all available time (3 points)
_____ left a little early (1 point)
_____ was one of the first to leave (0 points)

l) WRITE MY PAPERS:
_____ from several books, in more than one draft (3 points)
_____ from one main book, in one draft (0 points)

m) FINISHED MY LAST PAPER:
_____ few days ahead of deadline (3 points)
_____ night before deadline (1 point)
_____ missed deadline (0 points)

n) PROOFREAD MY PAPERS:
_____ usually (1 point)
_____ never (0 points)

o) LOOK OVER PROFESSOR'S COMMENTS ON GRADED PAPERS AND EXAMS:
_____ carefully (2 points)
_____ quick glance (1 point)
_____ just check out grade (0 points)

p) USUALLY STUDY:
_____ at my own desk or in a quiet part of the library (3 points)
_____ in a study area where I can meet friends (1 point)
_____ on my bed or in a soft chair (0 points)

q) PRACTICED STUDYING TEXTBOOKS BY THE "SKIM, READ, REVIEW"
   TECHNIQUE:
_____ more than once (3 points)
_____ tried it once (1 point)
_____ didn't bother (0 points)

r) VISITED A LEARNING CENTER OR WRITING WORKSHOP:
_____ yes (1 point)
_____ no (0 points)

s) WORKED ON INCREASING MY READING SPEED:
_____ yes (1 point)
_____ no (0 points)

t) PUT INTO ACTION ANOTHER SUGGESTION IN THE ACADEMIC SECTION
   OF THE BOOK:
_____ yes (5 points)
_____ no (0 points)

_____ TOTAL OF CHECKED ITEMS

RESULTS:

40 - 50   Congratulations. You have been paying close attention.

30 - 39   Reread some sections and put the tips into practice next term.

0 - 29   Get serious and quit wasting your time!

Investigate why you won't take advice.

23. HANG IN THERE, BABY

Here's a way of responding to the frustrations of being a college student. One guy would turn the volume all the way up on his stereo and bang his head against the wall so hard he dented the plaster. Far more common, and less painful, is to lock the door, lie on the bed for days, and wish the world would go away. The omnipresent question is always: "What am I still doing here?" When things get tough, lonely, or totally out of control sit down and answer that question for yourself.

The professions are closed to anyone without a degree, as are the salaried career-track jobs. There is still opportunity for entrepreneurial types without degrees, or for artists, writers, skilled workmen, technicians, and so on. But, ours is a society that rewards credentials.

That is what lies behind the often asserted statement that a college degree is worth big money in the long run. The most optimistic figure we've seen comes from Dr. Anthony Patrick Carnevale, an economist with the American Society for Training and Development. He compares the overall lifetime earning potentials of two students: the first not having completed high school, and the second with a college degree plus some further adult education. Dr. Carnevale estimates the extra degrees add $631,000 more income over the years.

If you are the first in your family to attend college, the stakes are very high. The degree will be your main chance to make a major leap economically and, in many ways, socially. Jack Kemp said, "America is shedding its industrial skin." If he's right, the days of high-paying entry-level blue-collar jobs will not return. Statistics show that families headed by college graduates have increased their real earnings since 1980, while those headed by men or women with less than four years of college have lost real earnings.

The whole college experience serves as "basic training" to blend in easily with workmates and mix with bosses. Co-workers tend to listen to, and take seriously, the college graduate who uses written and spoken standard English properly. People climbing towards high prestige jobs usually end up conforming, like it or not. They take on the general outlook of those who have already made it, helped along by the sometimes painful conditioning college puts you through.

The advice — hang on in — also applies to kids growing up with all the advantages. Their friends will pass through the college experience and anyone who misses out on a degree will feel the lack ten years down the road. An assistant headmaster worked for the same prep school from which he graduated. Henry patriotically left his elite private college to fly for the Navy. Years after his military discharge Henry was still paying a price for not finishing that degree. The headmaster's post opened up from time-to-time, he was the best person, but he never got it. Why? Because every time his name was mentioned someone was sure pointedly to bring up his lack.

People do sort out the world into college and non-college, degree and non-degree. That sheepskin will be proof that you can set a goal, knuckle down to hard work, and succeed.
See next chapter.

24. IT TAKES AS LONG AS IT TAKES

College careers don't always proceed at the "standard" pace. Priorities, maturity, and interests change over time. It's good to be flexible and realize that a tentative plan, which looked fine one year, may not the next. This is why colleges make it easy to stay on longer or to return after a leave. Many students take five years to get the B.A. and more than two years for the A.A.

Experts recommend going straight through for the degree, but you may be considering taking time off. Keep it from being a spur-of-the-moment decision. It's not wise to spring it unannounced on the family. Having a plan you can present will go a long way toward convincing a parent that you are not a "failure" or an emotional wreck. Explain that taking action now is better than drifting.

One option is to leave college to take any kind of a job in a field in which you are interested. An architectural major could find something with a real estate developer. A marketing student should knock on the doors of retailing chains.

Working at low-level jobs scares students right back to college, fast as they can run. Future employers will not be concerned about the gap in schooling, so long as you supply a plausible reason. Opportunities for graduate or professional schooling will rarely be damaged when you return and finish out at the same, or a different college.

If you can afford it, another option is to go to school somewhere else for a term. Try to transfer elsewhere for a change of pace. The mechanics are simple, especially since there are hundreds of institutions that will accept you. Talk to your dean, and file for a semester or a year away. Nicki is someone who got plenty out of this option. She decided that continuing at her school in New York City was not for her. She took a leave of absence one spring to spend it at her father's alma mater, an exclusive and secluded New England college, planning on pushing through a permanent transfer later. She just *knew* her pinks, greens, and madras would be a perfect fit there.

The next fall, who should be walking along Broadway but Nicki, almost unrecognizable in a leather mini-skirt and terraced hair. "I hated everything about the college! Everyone looked, sounded, and acted just like me." Many people are happy when they leave the school they started at. In her case the smart move had been to take the leave, which made it easy to return when things didn't work out.

A semester abroad also will be liberating — new environment, new foods, lessened expectations about performance, parents far away. Costs vary tremendously, depending on which institution is running the program, so check carefully. Most colleges have a Director of International Studies, or someone with a similar title, who gives advice and helps out on budgeting.

Anita put in a year at Sienna, Italy, for $600 less than a year at her public college. Her divorced mother had mastered manipulating bureaucracies, making phone calls, and filling out financial aid forms for five college-age children. It can be done if you really want it enough.

LIFE STYLES OF THE FAILED, BUT FAMOUS, QUIZ

Starting off slowly does not ruin prospects for life. The following people overcame their difficulties and went on to success. This quiz is not for credit.

A.
* His entire schooling consisted of one year's attendance
* Defeated first try at Illinois legislature
* Failed reelection to Congress
* Became the 16th President of the US

B.
* Poverty prevented her from attending college or law school
* Ran unsuccessfully for Utah State legislature
* Ran unsuccessfully for Congress
* Became Treasurer of the US and first woman to nominate a presidential candidate

C.
* Graduated 21st in class of 39 at West Point
* Resigned army commission on charges of drunkenness
* Failed in farming and real estate
* Relieved from his command in the Civil War
* Became the 18th President of the United States

D.
* A mob attacked her father's new house in a restricted neighborhood
* Schooling consisted of half-day sessions; dropped out of college after two years
* Wrote first play by a Black woman produced on Broadway

E.
* Could not afford college in Missouri
* Weak eyes kept him out of military academies
* Haberdashery store in Kansas City failed
* Defeated for second term as county judge
* Became 33rd President of the United States

F.
* Flunked his only course on filmmaking
* Dropped out of college after one term
* Won Academy Awards for *Annie Hall*, including Best Picture and Best Director

A) Abraham Lincoln; B) Ivy Maude Baker Priest; C) Ulysses S. Grant;
D) Lorraine Hansberry; E) Harry S. Truman; F) Woody Allen.

25. IT'S NOT THE END OF THE WORLD: SUSPENSION OR EXPULSION

Usually there's plenty of warning when a student is in serious danger of flunking out. The standard course of events is that a bad semester leads to a meeting with the dean and to probable probation. Take this hint.

Three ways to improve the next semester are: (1) reduce the level of difficulty by taking introductory surveys or fewer courses; (2) work more effectively to waste less time; (3) read this book through to help with number 2. If it's too late to salvage the semester, request a voluntary leave before the ax falls. It is far better to have a transcript filled with a column of withdrawals than with failures.

Even flunking out is not the end of the universe. Some administrator, somewhere, will forgive past indiscretions to enroll another warm body. Community colleges and, especially, trade and technical institutions, will happily sign you up in a degree program. Never lie about an unhappy past record on your new application. Admission officers always check.

It's often possible to return to your old institution. Demonstrate proficiency and greater commitment in an "open enrollment" program which offers credit courses, in the evening. (Avoid non-credit courses, since they can't be applied to a degree program.) After you have shown you are more capable of doing work at your institution than before, reapply.

The problem for many students is not flunking out, but running out. That is, running out of money. Arrange for an extended leave, rather than just suddenly disappearing. Professors who are not notified give students failing grades. If the housing office is not notified it will charge for the whole semester, keeping the bill on file. Returning will be simpler if there is no mountain of left-over problems. A dean will help you file for leave. When your finances improve, apply without hesitation for readmission.

If you have always been short of cash for your education you are far better off pushing through and avoiding leaves. This sure is tough, but you will find it a better thing to do than to try to return after a break. You'll have trouble reassembling as good a financial aid package. Besides, you may not feel like going back to student life after the independence of being in the work force and having ready cash.

Suspension or failing out are not so catastrophic that they cannot be overcome. Realize that there is no stigma attached to temporarily withdrawing, taking a leave, or transferring elsewhere.

26. THE SIXTY-SECOND STUDENT

Answering readers' questions did not prove difficult, since we made them up ourselves. Keep those cards and letters coming.

RX FOR TEXTS

Dear Sixty-Second Student:
My textbook is so boring I can't stand to read it one minute more. Got any suggestions?

Sleepily yours,
N.P., College Town, PA

Dear N.P.:
We hate textbooks as much as you do. The way to keep up interest in a course is to locate *real* books or articles. A sympathetic professor will recommend alternative reading which he or she would approve. You will need to know what to look for in this reading. So, pick up the assigned textbook and skim the first and last lines of every paragraph to get its approach. Then think of how happy you'll be when the time comes to sell your textbook.

Encyclopedias, handbooks, and out-of-print textbooks may turn out to be better written than the one your prof originally assigned. Check to see if the department you are studying in has a reading room where old books are sent for peaceful retirement.

INSTANT RESEARCH PAPER: JUST ADD COFFEE

Dear Sixty-Second Student:
Help! I have an 8-10 page research paper due in fourteen hours and I haven't started yet. How am I going to get it done?

Desperately yours,
J.R., Berkeley, CA

Dear J.R.:
Here's a speedy technique which moves you directly from your sources of information to your paper when time is short.

Start by skimming through a current encyclopedia article for an overview (but don't dare mention it in your bibliography or footnotes). Work from five real books, or some long articles. Select quotes from *all* of them, to demonstrate the research your prof is looking for. Line up your books — next to your coffee pot — placing long slips of paper at the interesting pages you will later quote.

Select one of these books as the "key text" — usually the most current and comprehensive. This key text will be your main source of ideas. Its treatment of the topic will also serve as your model. Set up an outline and a thesis paragraph (one containing your principal conclusions) early in the evening. Stick with them, because within three hours of writing your brain will be fried.

Don't copy big chunks, word for word, from the key text and pass them off as your own creation, even if this helps cut down on work at 4:00 a.m. Instead, summarize and rewrite in your own words, carefully footnoting from the key text to indicate pages used. One note every two or three paragraphs will do the trick.

Locate two strong quotes from each of the other books and sprinkle in. Plan to place the best ones at the beginning and end of the paper. Hold each direct quote to a short paragraph. Make sure they are footnoted.

Start typing. Insert the thesis paragraph on the first page. There will be no time for a second draft, so get a full bottle of correcting fluid. Maybe two. On a separate pad keep track of the books (with exact page numbers) mentioned as you move along. By the time the sun rises you won't be up to loading your book bag, much less be able to remember where the material originated.

At 6:00 a.m. you will worry less and less about spelling, two-page paragraphs, or dropping all the rules of grammar. But you should. Keep on typing. If you end up with more white-out than ink on the paper and it looks lousy, have it photocopied on high-quality paper. The result will amaze you.

Before you hand the paper in, make sure all the parts (title page with prof's name spelled right, all pages numbered, bibliography, footnotes, etc.) are there. Edit lightly in pencil. The paper may be better than you think, because some people can only work to a tight deadline.

SEMESTER'S END OVERDRIVE

Dear Sixty-Second Student:

Hey man, I'm dying. Exams are next week and I was social chairman this semester. Will I be in college next year?

Quizzically yours,
P.D., Tuscaloosa, AL

Dear P.D.:

Decide which courses you can motivate yourself in to impress your professors with your stunning comeback. Make those office visits. Explain why you felt a sudden desire to come in before the ax fell. Be humble. Ask what extra work you could do. Then do it. It also looks like you have some all-nighters ahead of you. Do them right.

(continued next page)

Figure out what needs the most work. If the schedule allows for it, put in all-nighters forty-eight hours before the brutal exams. Then, the evenings before, review notes from the long sessions. Another quick review just before you walk in, and good luck.

Now to the mechanics. Don't pull them with friends, who will look just as bad and act just as sullen at 5:00 a.m. as you. You waste less time and they won't be constantly reinforcing your worries.

Avoid sugar. It gives a quick high, but the drop afterwards wipes you out. Caffeine is okay, but speed, beyond being bad for your health, leaves you strung out when exams roll around.

Take a real ten-minute break every two hours. If the exam is at 9:00 a.m., there is much to be said for sleeping from 6:00 to 8:00. You better have a loud alarm clock.

Can I Package Myself To Look Good?

Dear Sixty-Second Student:
I want to make a career in the visual arts. Teachers tell me I have the talent. My friends say wise up and join the 90's, because artists starve. Which way should I go?

Creatively yours,
L.M., Bozeman, MT

Dear L.M.:
Put together a portfolio as fast as you can. Have first-class slides and photos made of your work, while you still have access to low-cost campus services. Find a sympathetic faculty advisor who will be willing to help you polish up the portfolio. Register with specialized employment agencies in a big city, even if you have to visit and do it in person. Their personnel will give you a critique at no cost, and with no obligation. They might even get you a job, instead of your having to do it on your own.

Am I Crazy to Change My Major When I'm So Close?

Dear Sixty-Second Student:
I always assumed that working in my chosen field was going to be a lot better than dragging myself through school. After putting in a miserably boring summer of work in an internship I'm panicky about my major. Guess there's no way out, since I'm only one course away from completing the sequence and my parents and friends have heard so much about my big plans.

Disenchantedly yours,
F.P., Houston, TX

Dear F.P.:

You still might not be giving your chosen career a fair shake. Being a full-time employee with a stake in the future can be quite different from tentative explorations.

If your distaste for this one, of many possible careers, is genuine, sit down and rethink your options. Don't worry about any bragging you did. See if you have enough free credits to upgrade a minor into a new major. You may have to stay on for an extra term or year to escape the original choice. This could turn out better than committing yourself to an increasingly unhappy future. Take control now.

What Do You <u>Do</u> With A Liberal Arts Degree?

Dear Sixty-Second Student:

I am getting a liberal arts degree and worry I won't be able to do a thing with it. Am I doomed to a life of driving a cab?

Despondently yours,
A.C., Iowa City, Iowa

Dear A.C.:

Certainly not, although you might be giving up good tips. Congratulations for being a generalist, which means you've been taught how to learn. Americans are constantly changing jobs and forever need to retrain. Grads with highly technical degrees, whom you envy now, start with high salaries, but often reach a plateau quickly, unless they get into management. Statistics show that your kind hit their stride by mid-life and reach the highest salary levels.

The University of Virginia sent out a questionnaire to its liberal-arts alumni who had graduated over the last fifteen years. Most worked in law, medicine, financial services and education. The graduates reported a median salary of $30,000, with 21% earning $50,000 or more. One-third of the 2,000 graduates who responded said that their degree gave them a leg up in their career area.

For entry-level jobs with your degree, look at *Life After Shakespeare: Careers for Liberal Arts Majors* (Penguin, 1985), or *Liberal Arts Power: How To Sell It on Your Resume* (Peterson's Guides, 1985).

27. DO GOOD, BE GOOD

This is not Romper room. Miss June says "Do Be a Do Bee." It's not Frank Sinatra's "Do be, do be, do" either. Our title refers to the rewards of idealism, both personally and professionally.

Idealism is not a word much used in connection with careers today, but there always has been, and always will be, satisfaction in fixing up the world. Religious and humanitarian organizations are out there, caring for the elderly, feeding the hungry, and protecting refugees.

Even the most hardheaded employers like to see their people take part in organized charity or community work. They lend executives out to the United Way, organize blood drives, or contribute personnel and goods to charity telethons and auctions. These days, government expects the private sector to shoulder a greater load of social responsibility than ever before.

There's a great tradition of private charity in this country. Levi Strauss & Company — makers of 501 Blues — has as its credo a commitment to place social issues above profits. The Bingham family recently sold two Louisville newspapers to the Gannett Company on the condition that the new owners continued to contribute 5% of the profits to local charities. Employers both approve of, and appreciate, employees who have shown a commitment to service. These observations are not a cynical comment that doing good for the community has a cash payoff. It just might, but that's not the point.

If there is an unmet need, students respond. For information on volunteer jobs, get a copy of *Helping Out in the Outdoors* from the American Hiking Society, 1015 - 31st Street, N. W. Washington, D.C. 20007 (Telephone 703-385-3252). The National Student Campaign Against Hunger is located at 37 Temple Place, Boston, MA, 02111 (Telephone: 617-292-4823).

Idealistic interests can yield satisfying careers. Look at public service: social work, clinical psychology, nursing, nutrition, and special education. There are all kinds of opportunities in therapy. Job security is excellent for these classic service professions. Philanthropic foundations hire administrators for programs involving millions of dollars. The money and fringe benefits are good, especially with a Master's Degree.

There's room for more public-interest lawyers. A number of law schools now provide innovative reduced pay-back schemes for graduates who make this commitment. Teaching is making a comeback, on all levels. There are various legislative proposals to greatly increase the salaries for "master teachers" and raise the standards of the profession.

The Peace Corps still offers an opportunity for anyone with any major. If you have an agriculture degree, or one from an institute of technology, you will be especially welcomed. Same goes for the UN's Food and Agricultural Organization whose home base is Rome, Italy.

There's plenty of room to help others without having to take up a life of saintly poverty. You can do good and still pay off your loans.

THE LITTLE BOOK OF WORLD RECORDS

MOST STUDENTS IN A TELEPHONE BOOTH
Ohio State University takes the prize for the largest institution in America, with over 52,000 students. The State University of New York is the world title champ, with close to 350,000 enrolled, state-wide.

MOST UNGRATEFUL STUDENT
The Roman emperor Nero had his old teacher, the Stoic philosopher Seneca, executed on a trumped-up treason charge. It was probably the C in Latin that did it.

THREE GREAT TEACHERS WHO NEVER PUBLISHED
Socrates, Jesus, and the Buddha.

GREATEST QUOTE FROM A SELF-EDUCATED PERSON
"The chief wonder of education" wrote Henry Adams, "is that is does not ruin everybody concerned with it, teacher and taught."

SECOND GREATEST QUOTE
"Never let your schooling get in the way of your education." Mark Twain

THE TOP RATED TV SHOWS ON CAMPUS OVER THE YEARS
Dead tie between — General Hospital, David Letterman, MTV, Wheel of Fortune, Star Trek, and Gilligan's Island.

ODDEST BULL SESSION
Five days of nutty papers, parties, and frivolous goings on every year at the "Conference on World Affairs," University of Colorado at Boulder. Get your reservation in early.

GREATEST NUMBER OF HONORARY DOCTORATES
Father Theodore Hesburgh, recently retired president of Notre Dame University, has been awarded 120. Former record holder was U.S. president Herbert Hoover, with 99.

Continued next page

(Little Book of World Records, continued)

BEST ADVICE TO GRADUATES

"Poor is the pupil who does not surpass his Master," according to Leonardo DaVinci.

SLOWEST LEARNER

Charlemagne, the master of all Europe in the 10th Century AD, kept a little slate under his pillow to practice on at night, but never did learn to write.

Ph.D. WHO GOT THE FURTHEST SELLING PLATITUDES

Dr. Leo Buscaglia dreamed up Public Broadcasting lectures on Love and made a fortune writing books preaching the astonishing news that hugging feels good.

MOST INDEPENDENT STUDENTS

Italian students in law and medicine founded their own universities in the Middle Ages, ran the institutions, and hired the faculty. Teachers were permitted one day off for a honeymoon. Seems fair.

MOST HELP FROM MOM

Mary Pickney Hardy MacArthur accompanied her son Douglas to West Point, where she saw him nearly every day. He went on to become the general who conquered Japan during WWII, on his own.

LEAST HELP FROM MOM

The mother of Bolivia's dictator, Enrique Penranda, holds this record. She said: "If I had known my son was going to be president, I would have taught him to read and write."

GREATEST QUOTE FROM A GENIUS

"Education," said Albert Einstein, "is what remains when one has forgotten everything he learned in school."

FURTHEST OUT

Clown College (Run by Ringling Brothers in Venice, Florida); Hamburger University (run by McDonalds in Oak Brook, Ill.); The Evergreen State College (no grades for students and no tenure for faculty); Universal Life Church (Ph.D., or ministerial credentials, or sainthood — only $5.00 by mail).

28. THE ACADEMIC FAST TRACK

"Geeks," "grinds," and "wonks." Face it. These labels the envious pin on academic achievers are self-deceiving. The stakes are too high to be contemptuous of people who study to get the grades.

There is an academic fast track in any institution. This track, as we define it, is entirely about grades, not about knowledge or self-awareness. Top grades mean winning departmental prizes, and getting the best job offers.

Anyone serious about applying for advanced professional training or for funded fellowships has to think ahead. Grades are the major index of achievement to admissions offices, panels, and interviewers.

Contrary to wishful thinking that employers are not interested in students who "spend all their time studying," recruiters go after achievers.

Surprisingly, the grades and the best interviews often go to people who didn't do well in high school or who floundered around in their first semesters in college. A common pattern for this type of student is to be overwhelmed at first by the complexity of the new material and the competition. They typically use the summer after their first year to digest these lessons and come back that fall with a plan that succeeds. Interviewers and graduate admissions officers understand, and value, this big jump when they review a college graduate's transcript.

Geoffrey rowed hard on the freshman crew and studied hard but didn't distinguish himself in either area. He was interested in philosophy, but wanted medicine as a career. By June he faced up to the need to structure his next three years or not get anywhere. He stopped rowing, but didn't completely abandon friendships with ex-teammates.

The grades started picking up virtually immediately, because he left no wasted moment in his week. Geoffrey took a premedical concentration. He registered for the absolute minimum number of science courses required for admission to medical school, but keyed in like a mad dog on those he took. He majored in philosophy. Through cultivating the faculty and by entering and winning essay competitions, he ended up as the best regarded of the department's undergraduates. When he worked, he worked. No interruptions, or distractions, permitted.

His girlfriend accepted this because when he wasn't at his desk he was able to loosen up. In his senior year he won a two-year fellowship to Oxford University in England to study medical ethics. He graduated summa cum laude and Phi Beta Kappa. Harvard Medical School allowed him to defer until he finished at Oxford.

Sad as it is, achievers make choices. They stop hanging out with old floor mates and friends from home. Fast trackers seek people who are achievers themselves, and politely minimize contact with unproductive students.

STUDY TECHNIQUES REVIEW CHECKLIST
(or ... Where Did the Time Go?)

CHECK ONE CATEGORY ON EACH LINE:

YES	SOME-TIMES	NO	
____	____	____	I study in the same place each time.
____	____	____	The lighting at my desk is good.
____	____	____	My study space is free of distractions.
____	____	____	I don't accept calls or visits when studying.
____	____	____	People have been asked to be considerate.
____	____	____	I plan a weekly study schedule.
____	____	____	For each day I have a schedule.
____	____	____	Sessions are based on my concentration span.
____	____	____	No one subject gets too much time.
____	____	____	After study segments, I take short breaks.
____	____	____	When I can, I set up study groups.
____	____	____	I avoid last minute all-nighters.
____	____	____	After a long session, I give myself a reward.

- If you checked **yes** for most lines, congratulations!
- Checking off a number of **sometimes** means keeping these techniques in mind the next time.
- Lots of **no** answers? You are making your study time harder than need be.

29. MANAGING TIME IN THE FAST TRACK

The undergraduate who wants to become a high achiever learns to mimic the response patterns of the motivated graduate and professional student. These older students take a driven, disciplined view of the subject matter and of academic life. They train themselves to focus on work.

Adopting a pseudo-grad school approach for yourself while still an undergrad need not mean completely dropping friends, or extracurricular activities. Nondirected leisure time has great value for college students. It gives them the flexibility to change and grow at their own pace. What undergrads can discover through this leisurely process has much to do with real learning. Just schedule your time carefully to get everything in.

Buy three calendars: a large wall calendar to see the whole semester at one time, a desk calendar to cover the month, and a pocket calendar to deal with daily and weekly scheduling. One week into the term, list major deadlines for papers, exams, lab reports, and drop dates on the wall calendar. After looking this over, create your own, *earlier*, deadlines for papers and reports to break up bottlenecks and relieve pressure.

Transcribe all this information to the desk calendar, leaving space for reading assignments and appointments. Keep the pocket calendar, updated regularly, with you as a constant reminder. Train yourself to look at your calendars every morning.

Careful scheduling also means watching the workload. There is nothing wrong with the occasional gut course to relieve the pressure and offer variety. Just don't take a gut with a stupid title that is a dead giveaway to anyone reviewing your transcript. (Two gems from the Brown University catalogue: "The Realm of the Interhuman"; "Rock and Roll is Here to Stay.")

Maximize the quantity and the quality of your study time, but walk a fine line to avoid burnout. If you discover you aren't working well at night, think about getting up early in the day to study before class begins.

If you find yourself working or reading too smoothly, you may actually be drifting. To fight this tendency, become active. This transforms mental tasks into physical ones and keeps you on the mark. Argue with the author's interpretations, jot things down, and solve problems. Read sections aloud, no matter how silly this may sound to a roommate. Be sure you have the connection between labs and the theoretical classwork clear in your head.

The academic fast track is not for everyone. People who want to get on it almost always have a firm goal, the discipline to stick with it, and the capacity to work within the grading system, as it is. Winston Churchill pushed through the Royal Military College, Sandhurst, and three wars, including WWII when he was Britain's inspiring prime minister, by this belief: "There is no use in saying 'we are doing our best.' You have got to succeed in doing what is necessary."

AND NOW, A FEW WORDS FROM THE COACH

UCLA football coach, Red Sanders: *Winning isn't everything. It's the only thing.*

***

Notre Dame football coach, Knute Rockne: *Show me a good and gracious loser and I'll show you a failure.*

***

Arizona State football coach, Darryl Rogers: *They'll fire you for losing before they'll fire you for cheating.*

***

Nebraska football coach, Bob Devaney, on lifetime contracts: *I had a friend with a lifetime contract. After two bad years the university president called him into his office and pronounced him dead.*

***

Ohio State football coach, Woody Hayes: *We'd rather have an immoral win than a moral victory.*

Anyone who tells me "Don't worry that you lost, you played a good game anyway," I just hate.

Without any winners, we wouldn't have any godamn civilization.

***

University of Cincinnati football coach, Tony Mason: *The thing is that 90 percent of the colleges are abiding by the rules, doing things right. The other 10 percent, they're going to bowl games.*

***

Penn State football coach, Joe Paterno: *Winning isn't everything. I'll never buy that if a boy loses a football game, he's a loser in life. You'll never sell me that one in a million years.... When I was a kid and would come home after playing ball, my father would ask me, "Did you have fun?" That was it.*

***

30. PREPARATION IS EVERYTHING ON THE FAST TRACK

Go to *all* classes. There are only two exceptions. If you are sick or exhausted, take time off, because if you don't you'll get worse and so will your grades. The other exception is when classroom attendance is 100% useless. Cut when everyone recognizes that distributed notes or the readings cover absolutely everything delivered in the lectures and when there are no important audio-visual materials which have to be seen in person. Make sure to check regularly for changes in due dates and get new handouts. Any time freed up by cutting in a course like this should be converted to extra study time. Getting work done for other classes will minimize the disgust you will feel with a Mickey Mouse course.

When you are in class, sit up front and take careful notes. Question the professor and initiate discussions. Go up to the desk after class with an occasional comment. Departments and institutions generally give their prizes to students who have made themselves known.

Don't bring a tape recorder to class because everyone else is doing it, except in the most complex scientific lectures. Instead, learn to take notes faster. Check them out with fellow students, picking up anything missed.

For a student on the fast track there is no such thing as over-preparing for an exam. This means working and reworking lecture notes for clarity, as soon as possible after a session. Have more flashcards than Doritos. Set up a study group with other committed students, but if it degenerates into bull sessions drop out immediately.

On examination day, fast track students stay calm because they know they are fully prepared and won't let distractions throw them. In courses where there will be several examinations, fast trackers push to earn an A the first time out. Not only does this impress the professor early, but gives you the benefit of the doubt should you need leeway later on.

Papers are your main opportunity to shine, because strong writing is what impresses professors. No matter how it looks in the classroom, the job of lecturing often comes second to their deeper career interests in publishing articles. Fast trackers learn to touch type, or else line up a trustworthy typing service long before deadlines. Find someone to put the research paper onto a word processor, which makes it easy to rewrite.

Even if a professor will accept a handwritten paper, *always* give in a cleanly typed version to gain the extra psychological edge. Unlike exams, scheduling of papers and projects is fully under your control. Hand in your paper or project early, if your prof permits you to do so. If it doesn't go over, there will be time to review and resubmit.

Students on the fast track take advice. The campus is filled with people eager to offer guidance — librarians, professors, peers, chairpersons, counselors, deans, advisors, and tutors. Students who consult with *all* these people do sensationally well. In the end, what keeps achievers on the mark in college and career is that they listen.

II. SOCIAL LIFE

1. BUILD THE PERFECT ROOMMATE

The perfect roommate always keeps the refrigerator stocked. Never uses the last drop of shampoo. Loans you money and then forgets about it. Is never in the way, or in the room, except when typing your paper as a favor. Not only listens to great music but brings along a $3,000 stereo with 6-foot speakers. Cleans up, but is not obsessive.

Finding this person is like designing a perpetual motion machine. Can't be done.

You start having delusions the summer before the first term, when that fat packet arrives from college. Out tumbles a roommate request-and-information form. This questionnaire asks you what you are like and what you want in others — smoking/non-smoking, studious/partyer, rock'n'roll/classical. There's a temptation to exaggerate how studious, clean, and quiet you are in hopes of locating roommates who would make any mother proud. It's better to be accurate. Remember others play the same game.

A realistic goal is to have two or more individuals stay out of each other's way and get along. Some housing offices pass on addresses before the term starts, so that roommates can get in touch. A phone call or letter with some specifics about how to furnish the room smooths things out. No need to overload on stereo equipment or drag in two sofas.

Schools maintain dorms so that students will have a place to study and sleep. This is obvious, but worth mentioning, because roommates who interfere with either function are more than discourteous -- they are in violation of college and university by-laws.

Get the big issue — noise (specifically music) — out of the way before the term begins. Music so defines certain people that they think they have a right to have it whenever they want it, or all the time. No way. Then there are the noise-Nazis, who think that they should be able to hear a pin drop in their rooms on a Friday night. They have to be forced to learn tolerance. Don't hesitate to ask the RA to jump in.

A ready-made negotiation form is available for $1.00 from Roommate's Starter Kit, P.O. Box 973, State College, Pennsylvania 16801.

See next chapter.

ANXIETY PREVENTION CHECKLIST

This list mentions some of the common fears first-term students report during their initial encounters with college. Check off the ones you are experiencing or believe you might face.

- ☐ I might not have enough money to stay in school.
- ☐ I could have difficulty meeting new friends.
- ☐ I might become depressed and so not make good grades.
- ☐ College might be too difficult for me.
- ☐ I secretly fear I might not be "college material."
- ☐ I might disappoint my parents.
- ☐ I could have difficulty deciding on a major.
- ☐ I will probably become homesick.
- ☐ I worry that my old friends will think I have moved away from them.
- ☐ I am afraid I won't be able to understand the professors.
- ☐ I fear I am shy and will have to talk in class.
- ☐ Perhaps I am not as sophisticated as all the other students.
- ☐ I am worried that I don't know how to write.
- ☐ What if I am stuck in a tough science or math class?
- ☐ I'll be so busy I won't have time for sports.

DEALING WITH THE RESULTS.

It is better to get early fears out in the open and on paper so you can deal with them. Most of what you checked off will seem groundless to you in a few months, but it's better to know now what you want to work on. The passage of time and the acquisition of skills, maturity, and confidence will do wonders. You too will someday be a senior!

DEVELOP A STRENGTHS LIST.

Place your name in bold letters across the top of the page and next to it write: "My Strengths." Start listing the things about yourself that you really like, and don't leave out anything, no matter how trivial. Your list might include "very neat," "great sense of humor," "like to read," "reliable," "people usually like me," "strong backhand," etc.

When you finish the list, put it somewhere (like inside the top drawer of your desk) where you can look it over whenever you doubt yourself. So, instead of a focus on secret fears, you learn to put your best foot forward by setting out a positive self-image. Go for it.

2. SHARING SPACE —
THE FINAL FRONTIER

It can be infuriating to walk out leaving twenty bucks in $5 bills on your desk and return to find only $10, the rest having been borrowed to buy two six-packs and a bag of Cheeto's. Some folks, though, can't understand why people who live together get frazzled over small change, which is sure to be repaid, sometime or other. No matter which side of this touchy subject you are on, don't get mad — talk it through so it won't come up again.

Old habits cause more trouble than money. Some guys spend their college years living like absolute animals because they think that's the classic way to go. If you can't live like this, it's attitude adjustment time. We can't emphasize enough the importance of talking it out. It's the small stuff that drives people berserk. Not putting the cap on a tube of toothpaste has destroyed many a marriage, much less an artificial and enforced roommate situation. You'll have to come to an agreement about the shampoo, the laundry supplies, and the milk in the refrigerator.

Telephone bills, especially if you are homesick, are a huge problem. The phone company knows that the only way to get its money is to make one person legally responsible. If you're that person, post the bill each month and ask that others claim their calls. Unclaimed calls and service charges get split equally. Don't get conned into taking responsibility for the whole end-of-the-year bill. Assess roommates double their average monthly charge before they leave on vacation. Promise to reimburse them any overcharge, and carry through.

Use the same technique off campus for the last month's rent and utilities. This way, no one gets worked over. The person stuck with the big bills never sees checks over the summer, no matter how sincere the promises. Out of sight out of mind.

In the same way rules are set for bills, lay down a guest policy. Undergraduates are too easy on one another when it comes to tolerating miserable behavior. The "Us" (lovable students) against "Them" (nasty administrators) attitude lets aggressive personalities make suckers out of their fellow students, all in the name of freedom and defying authority.

No one should meekly give up the room every night for long periods, just because a roommate wants to be alone with a lover. As a courtesy, once in a while, this is a friendly gesture, but don't tolerate anyone taking in a lover as a permanent addition. You shouldn't have to put up with a constantly changing cast of characters marching through, either. Taking a stand against intrusion has nothing to do with judging another person's morality. It's only a matter of your rights. This applies equally to non-sexual situations, if strangers are constantly invading your room.

There are all kinds of combinations of people living together. Many roommates become great friends and remain close for years. Others simply live together, stay out of each other's way, and survive.

3. CARE AND FEEDING OF PARENTS

Parents of college students living away shouldn't have to put pictures on milk cartons or billboards to find out what happened to their kids. Not touching base is a misguided attempt at total independence in the day-to-day routine of your new life.

Days rush by. When you don't call home your parents get anxious. One mother started calling her daughter every other Sunday morning — at 8:30 a.m. — because she knew (hoped) her daughter would be in. She didn't care that her daughter wasn't up yet. If you'd rather sleep in late, schedule systematic times to call home. Collect calls are expensive so get a Personal Identification Number card from the phone company. This cost-saving option allows calls made to home to be billed directly to your parents.

Keeping in contact by postcard has a great advantage over a phone call. You don't have to answer embarrassing questions. Buy a dozen cards. Address and stamp them at the start of the term. When the mood strikes, send off one with a couple of lines saying how well everything is going. It's really not a good idea to ask for money *every* time.

Students who avoid contact with parents often do so out of anxiety. Too many parents have the notion that every conversation or letter should be an occasion on their part to pour on the pressure. "Get the grades ... Take the LSAT's ... Pledge my old fraternity ... Stay away from that bum, he's no good for you." The questions are endless: "What did you get on the biology test? ... How come we never hear about any girlfriends? ... More money, don't you have enough clothes already? ... What job can you get with that major?"

It's always easy to get a fight going with parents by throwing in some classic lines: "I just *knew* you wouldn't understand." "I don't want to talk about it." "What would you know about it, anyway?" Parents never appreciate snappy comebacks. That's a sure way to escalate tension.

Instead, adopt a negotiating strategy. Don't appear to be evasive. Stay calm and say less than usual. Learning to respond in a neutral way will save wear and tear on your nerves. Try: "Why do you think so?" "I see what you mean." "Why do you believe I should do that?" "Let me think it over."

Growing apart is a part of growing up. Calmly explain to your parents that every choice and every change isn't a personal attack on them. Parents always want to know how their children are doing. Give them more to focus on than grades. Shift the discussion to what you are actually learning from your teachers. Also, talk about whatever is going on outside of class.

Invite them to visit the campus. All schools have Homecoming, and some have Dean's functions specifically designed for relatives. The visit never turns out to be as horrifying as you fear, unless you insist upon introducing them to friends you know they will hate. Have them meet a professor who will say nice things about you, and they will go away happy.

By the way, don't expect your mother to be any more reasonable on campus than she is at home. She still won't let her baby go out in the rain without a hat.

See next chapter.

82

IT'S THE FAMILY MATCH GAME!

RULES: Match up a statement in the first column with a response from the second column to win big prizes.

PARENTS
(What they say)

1. Now when I was your age...

2. Your father and I pay a lot of money for your tuition.

3. Don't you dare talk back to me!

4. I'm sure your professor must have had a good reason for doing that.

5. College ruined you. You used to be so nice.

6. We always thought you had so much *potential*.

7. But you did so well in high school ...

CHILDREN
(What they say)

A. I don't want to talk about it now.

B. Oh, just forget it ...

C. I just *knew* you wouldn't understand.

D. Well, everything is so expensive.

E. How was I to know the prof was serious about it?

F. I don't care what happens.

G. It's too late to do anything about that course now.

(What you'd like them to say)

*   I love you no matter what.

*   I understand how tough it is.

*   I'm behind you 100% in this.

(What they'd like you to say)

*   I see what you mean.

*   Give me some time to think about it.

*   I might be able to do it that way.

4. MONEY FROM HOME: UNHOOKING OBLIGATION FROM AFFECTION

This book pays attention to grades, and should say why. Everyone knows that if the grades aren't there out you go, yet the most intense pressure often comes not from the college, but from parents. The same horror stories surface on every campus. Funds cut off. Love withdrawn. Twenty tons of guilt in a fifteen-minute phone call. Rumbles at Thanksgiving and eruptions at Christmas. What all students would like to hear is "I love you no matter what." Making tuition or affection conditional upon fulfilling expectations can rip up a kid's guts.

Teachers, deans, counselors, and even friends can reduce the tension with your parents. Jeff's life needed some fine tuning. It wasn't going so well at school or at home. One day his roommate made it down the hallway doubletime to fetch their resident assistant. Jeff's father was standing outside his son's door demanding to be let in. Jeff had been having trouble throughout his second year and his father was there to "talk some sense into the boy." The RA ended up spending an hour and a half on a bright Sunday afternoon preventing him from breaking down the door (school property, you know), getting Jeff to undo the bolt, and sitting down between the two to talk it out. Naturally, the RA wasn't able to solve the long-term misunderstandings, but she was able to convince Jeff's father that his grades weren't that bad for a student who had just made it in by the skin of his teeth.

No parental choice can dominate a person's career forever. You shouldn't give up all control over your destiny just because your parents are paying your way. Students find it difficult in these arguments to deal from a position of strength because they feel guilty about the cost of their schooling. No surprise. At the most expensive colleges classes are up to $40 a session. To inflict further torture, figure it out to the minute. So what? The typical American route to improving status is through college. Just because parents pay tuition does not mean their children have to be eternally grateful. Students too often undervalue the contribution they make to their own education through scholarships, grants and money from their jobs.

It's tough for parents to give up control. Relying on them to support you through college drags out your adolescence. One way to become an adult is to stop being critical of your parents for being critical of you. Make the move from mere tolerance to affection or it will be a heavy burden for you to carry through life. You do this as much for your own long-term well-being as to ease life with your parents right now.

Breaking through the ice may mean drawing up a little list (which should be kept private) about the things you most *like* about your parents. When was your mother particularly insightful or sensitive? When was your father a help and a guide? While making up this list forget about squabbles. Forcing yourself to feel positive about your parents will lead to letting them know that they're loved, even if this is something "not done" in your family. Better now, than never.

5. A THOUSAND STRANGERS: LONELINESS DOESN'T LAST

Take a group of strangers, uproot them from their home environment, and throw them together in a competitive atmosphere. Have this happen during a time of emotional instability and intense nervous excitement. There you have it — the First Year. No surprise that surveys show 18- to 20-year olds have the highest levels of loneliness of any age group. Beginners in college are displaying what psychologists label "situational loneliness." Fortunately, it gets better fast.

For most residential students, "situational loneliness" is just garden-variety homesickness. Lots of kids never went away to summer camp, and rarely so much as spent a week-end away from their room. Although things may be tough at first, they improve rapidly. At the University of Iowa, while 52% of first-year students reported being lonely at the beginning of the year, almost all who stayed adjusted by the spring semester.

Still, it's not easy to ignore that first dose of homesickness. It makes many a student run back to the old comfortable situation. Sally left a small town in Ontario, Canada, with her best friend, June, and headed for a college in Michigan. They had "matching everythings" planned for their room. When they arrived they covered the walls with cute posters, and filled the shelves with fuzzy animals.

The first sign of trouble came when Sally signed up for morning classes and June registered for afternoon sessions, because she liked to sleep in. June would wake up, find herself alone in the room, and cry. Sally would return to an empty suite, and cry. When they finally got together every night they would sob disconsolately about how much they missed their boyfriends, families, and hometown.

Three weeks into the term, Sally and June rolled up the posters, gathered all the cuddly critters, tossed everything into a big box, and fled. June married her high school sweetheart a few months later. When Sally got home she took a long look around and rethought her life. She broke off with her old boyfriend and enrolled the next fall in a new school. Her main regret now is that she lost a year by not sticking it out the first time around.

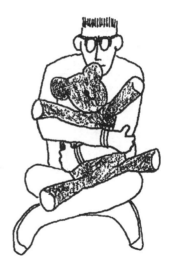

(continued next page)

85

The common reaction of people to a new and fearful situation is inertia. They sit around hoping something will happen. At a residential college the first persons you meet are floormates. Introductions are automatic at first, but if you don't respond positively the flow of introductions dry up. There has to be a show of enthusiasm. Offering free food is the ultimate enticement. Anyone who springs for a donut break or orders in a couple of pizzas to their room will find their floor covered with wall-to-wall spongers.

New commuters should absolutely join an organization to break out of isolation. If you go to meetings but sit silently you are no better off. Plan to say one thing in public at the second meeting, and occasionally thereafter. That's the only way to get known, and to have people want to meet you.

See next chapter.

TV OR NOT TV? —
THERE IS NO QUESTION

You may have watched a whole lot of TV at home, but don't set up your wide-screen projection color set or little black and white in your room because:

- College is the only place in the whole world where TV is not important and will get in your way. Older professors did not grow up with the tube. A lot do not even own a set, believe it or not. Even those who watch TV won't be following the shows that interest you.

- It will not help you in your classes. College is dominated by books, not electronic images. Your profs will not appreciate any references to TV.

- Why hide out in your room? There are sets on floors and in lounges to watch David Letterman or *General Hospital*. This is a way to meet people. Anyway, there is just too much entertainment going on all over campus for you to put in your usual heavy time in front of the box.

- Unlike high school, the next day everyone will not be discussing the same show you saw, unless it was a Super Bowl.

- Think of those extra hours you will have to study if you cut off *all* TV! At least, go on reduced rations until you graduate.

6. A SMALL CIRCLE OF FRIENDS

In every college town there's a row of bars with Michelob neons in the window and Bud Lite decals on the door. A good place to meet new people? Not really. They are guaranteed to be noisy and crowded. Party bars are for groups of friends to go off in search of other groups of friends.

Getting smashed in bars, at big parties, or during beer blasts feels like socializing, but is often just a different way of avoiding real contact. Smaller, more personal, parties where the music and energy level are not so frantic provide a better setting for conversation.

Don't always wait for a party situation. There will be moments after class, on the line at the bookstore, or on the bus home, when there are interesting people all around ready for you to meet. Colleges set up locations where conversation is encouraged. In a poorly designed institution students seize on spaces they make their own: a dorm hallway or a floor in a corner of the undergrad library. For practice, talk to one new person each day.

Even at a party campus, you can make intellectual friends, if that is what you want. Listen to what students say in class and then follow-up with the bright ones after the session.

It's tough to get started, but fellow students are approachable, even if they haven't learned to give that impression yet.

Here are some less than dazzling conversation openers, (beyond the "Hello, my name is _____. What's yours?" Which isn't that bad a way to go): "What was the teacher talking about?" "Can you believe how noisy this library is?" "Do you like that book?" "Amazing, the bus isn't here yet."

Then what? Once you psych up the courage to say something, and get a response in return, the easiest way to keep the ball rolling is to ask a personal question. Everyone likes to talk about themselves: "What dorm do you live in?" "Where did you go to high school?" "What's your major?"

Come off friendly. Smile and look at people's faces. Simple stuff, but mighty effective. Learn names. We are all so nervous when we meet someone we often do not quite hear a new name. Ask for the name again, to get it straight. Use the other person's name frequently. This will work out fine, because everyone appreciates the personal touch.

Really shy people won't find much of this helpful. The shy remain isolated, afraid to seek help and advice, because they believe others don't take their problem seriously. Shyness *is* a terrible handicap, especially because it can make you seem self-satisfied or cold, when you're actually anxious for contact.

The very shy have to think one-to-one. People who have been on their own develop a hobby, such as model building, sketching, photography, or hiking, to help them fill their time. Use this skill to meet a like-minded person. Make a quiet approach about your interest to one sympathetic fellow student in a hobby club, a dorm, or a class. This way, you don't have to talk about yourself, but about a subject. This should help build your confidence.

7. STALKING THE SIGNIFICANT OTHER

Don't know much about History
Don't know much Biology
Don't know much about a science book
Don't know much about the French I
took
But I do know that I love you
And I do know that if you would love me
too,
What a wonderful world this would be!
"(What A) Wonderful World"*

Sam Cooke's classic R&B hit from the 50's lays it on the line — love is vital. But where can you find someone?

She's in the library looking for any chance to avoid reading the textbooks in front of her. He's in the cafeteria, with nothing to do but chase peas around his plate. They're both hoping for company.

Lounges, bus stops, and lines, lines, lines, are filled with people bored out of their minds, dying for someone to come over and rescue them. These ordinary places are great because everyone has to be there. No one had to psych themselves up to go there. Nobody expects an act or a hustle. It's easier to make contact in a laundry room on a Wednesday afternoon than in a campus pub on a Friday night. The lower the pressure, the more naturally and smoothly things progress.

The classroom has the highest romantic potential of any place on campus. Students get tossed together a few times a week. What could be more natural than to go up to an interesting person and start talking. There's nothing easier than asking to borrow someone's notes on the way out of class. When they're returned, offer to buy a cup of coffee in exchange for the help.

That's easier said than done. Most of us are fairly shy and find it tough just to launch into a casual conversation. So look for emotionally charged situations as a way to break the ice. Drama, music, and dance groups make this their specialty. There's plenty to talk about as the tensions build up, or during the giddy post performance high. Newspaper and radio staffs develop similar bonds in the rush to get out the product.

Joining a religious or ethnic group helps. There's always a youthful, electric leader around just dying to introduce the flock to each other. Students who are lonely should let the leader know this because he or she will be unfailingly sympathetic.

8. THE DATING GAME

Everyone is nervous on a first date. Women worry about what they should wear or how they should behave. Men often go overboard trying to pull off an impressive evening.

There are many events on campus that are every bit as good as an expensive restaurant dinner. Speaking of food, there is nothing like a home-cooked meal by candlelight to impress somebody. A sophisticated date can cost little. Try last -minute student rush seats at a symphony concert. Think about late night espresso coffee and pastries at the top restaurant in town. This won't cost as much as a pitcher and a pizza with everything, but it's sure more romantic. After the first few dates, splitting costs is the relaxed way to go.

Not all women will ask a man out for the first date. Many women prefer to drop hints, instead, hoping that the clues will be picked up. According to a study conducted at Texas A & M, men often misinterpret being asked out on a date as a sexual invitation. The two female researchers who wrote the report were emphatic that when a woman asks a man out she must make it absolutely clear what's going to happen. Her hints have to be unambiguous and directed toward what she *really* wants.

The '80s left young people with an intense fear of graduating from the certainties of college social life into the uncertainties of the adult singles scene with its bars, computer dating, and personal ads. Many students rush to give up on random dating, especially when they see the end of their college career on the horizon.

Stability has gained in importance.

Carol was a great looking, two-sport varsity athlete. Her father was a well-respected neurologist, and over the years she had picked up the impression from her mother that there was much to be said for marrying an equally stable man who knows where he is going. Carol was talking with some friends during the fall of her senior year about the Harvard-Yale study that said a college-educated woman's likelihood of marrying dropped fast after the age of 25. After the age of 35 there is a slim chance that a woman will tie the knot. The now controversial and disputed report was all over magazine covers.

One of her friends said that obviously there's no better place to meet eligible men than right here at school. Carol was up front about what she wanted — an athletic guy of her background who was planning to get into either medicine or law. One friend looked up and said she ought to meet Fred. Carol was a June bride! Not everyone is *that* focused. The college dating game sometimes leads to immediate marriage, but it doesn't have to.

The relationship we know best is the one we've been watching all our lives — that of our parents. If you want to get serious about another person you should find out exactly what the emotional life of their parents is, or was, like. If they bickered, fought, or were cold to each other, the person you are interested in is likely to duplicate that experience in their own relationship. If your potential partner's parents were loving and supportive of each other, that is what their child expects in his or her own match up.

9. SEX

College students think about sex all of the time. After all, they're long past puberty and are surrounded by potential partners. What else is there to daydream about in a stuffy library?

Expending all that thought power on sex generates plenty of anxiety. Experts say: be natural, relax, and take it slow. Men worry too much about their performance level. When the University of Texas at Austin started a pre-recorded telephone hot line, the most popular tape (out of 150 subjects) was "Timing Problems in Male Sexuality." After a late session of heavy drinking and uncertainty about how an evening might end, men sometimes suffer temporary impotence or premature ejaculation. Women are more sympathetic to these problems than men think, and are usually willing to try again after a while, or at another time.

Consent is a very big issue for women. "How to say No" ranked high for the number of UT call-ins. Female counselors recommend a woman watch her step when accepting a ride or an invitation to an apartment from a man she doesn't know well. If he really likes her he will be willing to meet her another time or at a more public place. Female counselors say that if women are verbal about what they want and what their limits are, they have a better chance of avoiding trouble.

The consent issue for men is more complicated than it first appears, because they are still taught by society to be sexually aggressive. The rule is not to use or be used. Physical force or verbal intimidation equals date-rape, no matter how it is falsely justified then, or later.

That's worth repeating. The important point for both men and women is not to exploit and not to be exploited. Talk it out and take nothing for granted. No one has to do anything they don't want to do, nor should another person force anything upon a partner.

Men have an equal responsibility with women in preventing pregnancy by always using a contraceptive. This also helps for avoiding disease. If partners are not totally sure of one another's sexual history, a man should always wear a condom, no matter what birth control device a woman uses.

When men and women get realistic about sex the personal frustration level drops, and they become more comfortable. A study from Ithaca, New York, of over 500 undergraduate men and women rated factors that were important to them, in purely sexual situations. The men were interested in physical characteristics — attractiveness, facial features, buttocks, weight, legs, breath, skin, and breast size — in that order. It took more than fine physical features to interest women. They selected over-all attractiveness, sexuality, warmth, personality, tenderness, gentleness, sensitivity, and kindness. Obviously, body part preferences didn't count for much with these women.

No surprise, but when it came to the qualities both sexes were looking for in choosing *long-term* partners, the results of the Ithaca study were strikingly similar for men and women. Both sexes wanted honesty, personality, fidelity, sensitivity, warmth, kindness, character, tenderness, patience, and gentleness. So, at the point of getting into a serious relationship even men shift criteria from the purely physical to include the emotional. Statistics prove this over and over again.

A study of 1200 men and women conducted at Loyola University at Chicago show that persons with a high need for intimacy consistently reported a greater sense of well-being, were happier, and felt more secure than those lower on the measure. Another study, by the same researchers, looked at Harvard graduates from the 1940's classes. The higher the desire for intimacy the participants expressed while in their 30's, the more successful they found their jobs and lives were at age forty-seven.

Check out the Sixty-Second Student section for other specific info on sexual matters.

P.S.: One of the best known and most popular books to browse is Alex Comfort's illustrated, *The Joy of Sex.*

RITES OF PASSAGE

UNIVERSITY OF MICHIGAN: **Nude Run**. A mob of naked students — some wearing ski masks — makes a mad dash on the last day of classes from one end of the campus to the other. At the end, the runners pose for their "official" photo in front of the University's Museum of Art. Not an authorized Olympic sport.

ATLANTA UNIVERSITY: **Step Show**. Every Fall and Spring the fraternal organizations get together for exhibitions of dance or acrobatic steps passed on through each frat and sorority. Big crowds cheer on the competitors, who may pick up prizes. Go for it.

OBERLIN COLLEGE: **Mock Students**. The fledgling musicians' rebellion against black-tie formality and the recital process, held during the break before exams. It's an irreverent variety show where students parody classical and modern music while wearing shorts and swim suits, smash instruments, and mock-out their teachers. Roll over Beethoven.

CALIFORNIA INSTITUTE OF TECHNOLOGY: **Ditch Day**. On a given day in the Spring term, seniors leave the campus, first locking their dorm doors with weird contraptions that first-year students must solve to enter the rooms. Once the break-and-enter is carried off, the intruders must booby-trap the rooms to make it hard for the rightful occupants to get back in. Knock knock. Who's there?

PEPPERDINE UNIVERSITY: **Midnight Yell**. Every night during finals week, students throw open their windows and scream to relieve tension. Faculty and administrators serve as waiters and clear dishes at special midnight snack breaks. Non-credit Primal Scream Therapy.

FREDONIA COLLEGE: **Freedonia-Marxonia**. To honor the four Marx Brothers for their film *Duck Soup*, set in the mythical kingdom of Freedonia, students stage contests for the best impersonation, judge edible and non-edible versions of duck soup, show the film, and indulge in a mass photo as Groucho look-alikes. "But Professor Quackenbush, where will the students sleep?" "In the classrooms, where they always sleep."

UNIVERSITY OF PUGET SOUND: **Foolish Pleasures**. The short films which students make about their education at the institution are shown at a sham Academy Award night. The "producers" arrive in stretch limos, and the best film is granted a "Golden Camera" prize. And the Oscar goes to ....

SPAULDING UNIVERSITY: **Running of the Rodents**. The week before the Kentucky Derby race, students trot out eight rats they have carefully trained to run around a miniature version of Churchill Downs. Mint julep, anyone?

SAME-SEX RELATIONS

Does having an occasional fantasy, being involved in an adolescent crush on a member of the same sex, or even having some sexual contact mean that a person is gay or lesbian? Here's help. Sol Gordon, a psychologist specializing in sex education, offers a useful definition that sorts out those who probably are, from those who certainly are not, homosexual: "Someone who — *as an adult* has a *constant definite* sexual preference for those of the same sex."

It's not uncommon for students who had a definite homosexual preference in high school to try out a new, possibly more public, role in the freedom of the college environment. There are support groups on larger campuses that break isolation, while guaranteeing anonymity. It's no one's business how a student lives his or her sexual life. Some gays and lesbians will come out for personal reasons or because they see it as a political statement, but others won't.

Telling parents is always tough. Gays and lesbians who would like to explain their preference to their families, can look for advice and support from a local chapter of Parents and Friends of Lesbians and Gays Group. Look in the telephone book, or send a self-addressed, long envelope for the booklet "Coming Out to Parents" (P.O. Box 24565, Los Angeles, California 90024, or P.O. Box 15711, Philadelphia, Pennsylvania, 19103).

Students near larger cities might encounter appropriate partners at gay and lesbian bookstores, and affinity groups. The health crisis brought on by AIDS means a young man in gay life has to be extremely cautious regarding the physical aspects of sexuality. It's now a matter of life and death to practice safer sex. This means always using latex condoms and avoiding the exchange of bodily fluids, such as semen or blood. For more information, call the National HIV and AIDS Information Service (1-800-342-AIDS).

The ideal of uniting sexuality to intimacy in an atmosphere of mutual respect has a lot going for it. Not exploiting or being exploited is as good a rule for gays and lesbians as for heterosexuals.

FENDING OFF SEXUAL HARASSMENT

High-status males in our society generally assume that they deserve physical access to the young and sexually appealing, and society is much more accepting of older-man younger-woman combinations than their reverse. Secretaries, flight hostesses, waitresses and similar folk have long had to deal with this problem; and female students are in the same boat. Sometimes the approach is so oblique and indirect that you really don't know how to cope with it. The prof may come on fatherly, for example, or assure you that he is only concerned to free you from psychological inhibitions.

If any of this begins happening, you should withdraw promptly and firmly and drop the class. If there are grading problems or other academic issues at stake, talk to your advisor or someone you trust in the culprit's own discipline. Faculty members usually know each other's reputations on this score. Remember that you have an absolute right to protect yourself from sexual exploitation. Indeed, we increasingly have laws which forbid sexual harassment on the job or in schools. Women faculty will probably tend to help you in these difficulties, and so will any feminist groups on your campus.

Source: Inge Bell, *This Book is Not Required*. (The Small Press, 18603 Highway 1, Suite 15, Fort Bragg, CA 95437), p. 33.

10. THE SIXTY-SECOND STUDENT

Answering our readers' toughest questions was no problem, since we made them up ourselves. Keep those cards and letters coming.

Why Don't My Relationships Ever Last?

Dear Sixty-Second Student:
I'm a sophomore who has gone through several boyfriends. I met a guy during October I'm crazy about. Here it is almost finals week and he just gave me the routine about cooling things off. What's wrong?

Unhappily yours,
A.B., New Orleans, Louisiana

Dear A.B.:
Timing is everything. Statistics show college break-ups follow a cycle. There are three peak times. September, when the term begins, the end of the year, when everybody heads home for the holidays, and May, when the school year ends. Students with doubts use these natural breaks in the schedule to ease out of a relationship. A great deal of experimentation takes place on a campus. Anyone as successful as you've been in meeting men will meet more. At some point, things will click.

Doesn't No Mean No?

Dear Sixty-Second Student:
I have a friend who went through an incredibly upsetting and painful experience. She and this guy went out on their second date and stopped by his dorm to pick up more money. Once they were inside his room he made a pass and then forced himself on her. She's been feeling awful ever since. I say what he did was criminal, and she has nothing to be ashamed about.

Sincerely yours,
E.B. Chicago, IL

Dear E.B.:
This is a textbook case of "date rape." It doesn't make any difference if she was attacked in a deserted alleyway, or if what happened took place with someone she knew well. It's still rape. She bears no blame. Counseling will help her get over any misdirected feelings of guilt that she encouraged him, or remorse that she went to the room in the first place.

(continued next page)

Let your friend know that she's hardly the only woman on a campus who's been forced into sex against her wishes. A study at Auburn University revealed that college men engaged in a wide-range of practices that are coercive. Sixty-one percent had placed a hand on an unwilling woman's knee or breast, and forty-two percent had removed or disarranged a woman's clothing against her will. A full fifteen percent of the 190 males in the study acknowledged they had had intercourse with a woman against her will.

To head off problems, women should become aware of attitudes certain men carry with them. A study at Texas A & M pointed out that men regarded having sex against a woman's wishes as more justifiable if the man always pays for everything, or if the woman asked the man out, or if they go right to his apartment on the first date. Charlene L. Muehlennard summarized her colleagues' findings: "We are not suggesting that a woman should not initiate a date or go to a man's apartment. We do feel that it's important for women to know that such actions might be misinterpreted by men."

How Can I Cut Down on Overload?

Dear Sixty-Second Student:
When I bought my car I thought it was going to be great. I hated taking the bus. The problem is, I never figured in all the heavy extra costs. Moving out of my folks' house and into my girlfriend's apartment was also going to be great, but I have to put in more hours at my job because we've been spending a lot. She tells me that if I go to school part-time my grades will go up again and, besides, I'll have more time to be with her. I'm not too sure about cutting back on school, but maybe she's right. What do you think?

Exhaustedly,
W.H., Buffalo, NY

Dear W.H.:
Sounds like you have a serious case of overload. School work is so tough that it's guaranteed to suffer when you pick up too many other responsibilities. If you keep expanding your working hours you'll drop out. Sad but true. Never let the cash from a part-time nowhere job make you lose sight of that diploma.

Start cutting back. Get rid of the car. Move closer to campus. If your friend can't figure out that you have to be fresh in the morning for school and must put in the study hours late at night, this is a sure sign your goals are different from hers. Don't kid yourself. It's time to make some decisions.

A Little Bit Pregnant?

Dear Sixty-Second Student:

I've been on this campus for three months and I can't believe how ignorant people are about their sexuality, and *especially* about birth control. Can you believe that some kids think that a girl won't get pregnant if it's her first time! Are these people out to lunch or what?

Name and College Withheld
Upon Request

Dear Name:

Unfortunately, your college is probably no different from the rest. A Gallup Poll survey of 100 campuses nationwide revealed that although the majority of respondents claimed to be sexually active, most were poorly informed. As many as 32% believed that if a male withdraws just before ejaculation this fully protects a woman from pregnancy. Dead wrong. Few women on "The Pill" were aware of the lower dose mini-pill (progestin only) which is a major health advance. More than 20% thought it was "dangerous" to have sexual intercourse while the woman was menstruating. Dead wrong, again.

Sixty-five percent of unwed mothers are over 20 years old, so this is not just a teenage issue. Here are some facts. Sexual partners have to use contraceptives *every time*. It's not unromantic to use birth control devices, or to talk about them before engaging in sex. Many campuses have clinics which dispense pills, fit women for diaphragms, and offer advice. Women who do not have this service on their campus can call the local Planned Parenthood Office, or locate a sympathetic gynecologist.

The prevention rates, in descending order, for various methods [adopted from *Family Planning Perspectives Journal*] are:

Condom (combined with vaginal foam)	99%
Norplant	99%
The Pill*	97-95%
I.U.D. (virtually off the market now)	95%
Condom alone	90%
Cervical cap	87%
Diaphragm (with spermicide)	81%
Sponge (with spermicide)	90-80%
Vaginal chemicals (alone)	82%

*Women who smoke should realize this reduces the effectiveness of The Pill. Use of The Pill increases the chance of getting Chlamydia Trachomatous infections. Therefore a woman who is sexually active with more than one partner should ask these men to use condoms to prevent trading this infection.

(Continued on next page)

(A Little Bit Pregnant?, continued)

Methods with a very low prevention rate are:

Coitus interruptus (withdrawal)	77%
"Rhythm method"	76%
Douche	60%
Leaving it to chance	10%

Couples who are conscientious and cooperative about using contraceptives every time rarely have unwanted pregnancies.

"I Can't Get No Satisfaction...."

Dear Sixty-Second Student:

Why haven't I found the woman of my dreams? Where are the campus sex goddesses I was panting for all through high school? It's still the same old romantic crap with these women — commitment, feelings, and all the rest of that BS. What gives?

Disgustedly,
B.E., Milwaukee, WI

Dear B.E.:

Wise up. You have distorted expectations. The male magazine industry creates and feeds these fantasies. *Playboy* has always made the college market a target. It does back-to-school issues, draws up all-star collegiate teams, and does photo features entitled "Girls of the Big Ten." There never has been a woman in the magazine with blemishes, bulges, or wrinkles. At the dream factories, photographers, make-up people, and photo retouchers work overtime to make sure that reality never intrudes.

Penthouse also gets a large college readership, particularly for its lunatic letters. Postmen routinely encounter naked housewives, and students are forever jumping into bed with their roommate's sisters (both of them). It's a land where the time between the first encounter and sex never takes longer than five minutes.

The basic delusion is that perfect women are always available. No emotional involvement is necessary on anyone's part. Looking at too many photographs leads to dissatisfaction with real women. The first step towards getting back on track is to stop believing everything you read by guys named Hugh or Bob.

What Do I Need to Know About Safer Sex?

Dear Sixty-Second Student:

I'm getting tired about hearing that sex is bad for you. It seems every time I browse the magazine racks in the college bookstore there is a cover on a magazine about the horrors of some sort of sex disease. I feel safer in a college situation than I would if I were making the singles bar scene. I like sex and want some information so I don't have to panic. How do I reduce the risk of catching something?

Cautiously yours,
P.V., Athens, Georgia

Dear P.V.:

Be straightforward with your partners by asking if they're healthy, before getting into bed. There are times when your partners will not be honest, or are ignorant of their own symptoms. In bed, be suspicious if you see sores, discharges, rashes, or warts. It's never too late to call it off.

Certain forms of venereal disease (VD) — also called sexually transmitted diseases (STD) — are on the rise, while some others are showing reduced rates. Infections to be most concerned about are gonorrhea, syphilis, herpes, and, of course, AIDS.

A new condom (rubber) should always be used. Only buy ones made in the U.S. A condom lowers the risk of infections for both partners only if used from start to finish. Putting on a condom for the first time does take getting used to. A little practice in private helps. Any slight reduction in pleasure is more than compensated for through the relaxation which comes from safety. Beyond this mechanical protection, restricting sex to trustworthy partners is the biggest plus.

A check list provided by the American Social Health Association lists signs which could mean infection: burning when you urinate/ discharge from your sex organs/ sores and bumps on or around the sex organs/ itching in or around the sex organs/ unexpected rashes/ cramping or unexpected stomach ache (especially in women)/ bleeding from the vagina at times other than a normal period.

The symptoms of venereal disease are especially confusing to women. The damage may be hidden inside their body or mistaken for normal female discharge. Instead of worrying, both women and men should visit the doctor. Your diagnosis will be confidential. If your campus does not have a clinic, call the toll-free Sexually Transmitted Disease National Hotline (1-800-227-8922) for the location of a free or low-cost clinic. STD happens to nice people too. It is also preventable.

Can the Campus Nourish My Spiritual Life?

Dear Sixty-Second Student:

I love my large, diverse, campus. I've been trying to convince my parents to let me stay. They argue it will destroy my faith. I don't want to go back to live with them again, or have to go to a different school.

Nervously yours,
L.G., Norman, OK

Dear L.G.:

Reassure your parents by letting them know you regularly attend your house of worship. Have your pastor, priest, or rabbi drop them a line about you. Some slipping just comes from neglect. Hooking into a campus religious organization will keep personal convictions strong.

You may also have to explain to your parents that freedom of religion in America means the right to have a faith, or to have no religion at all. Students learn to be respectful of intellectual diversity in the classroom. So too, they become tolerant about religious difference of opinion. A give-and-take of discussions on a non-denominational campus stretches the mind and can enrich personal faith in the end.

Fun and Games: Athletics

Dear Sixty-Second Student:

I've been feeling very tired lately, even though I'm getting enough sleep. I'm just sort of dragging myself from class to class. What can I do to get out of this rut?

Yawningly yours,
D.D., Miami, Florida

Dear D.D.:

Sounds like what you need is a quick infusion of adrenalin. Run, swim, bike, or cross-country ski on your own. Play tennis, squash, handball, or racquetball with a friend. Lift weights for bulk, for tone, or for fun. Join an intramural team, or if you are really in the mood for a change, look around for a sport that takes walk-ons. Lacrosse, rowing, fencing, and rugby are distinguished, if little played, sports. Enroll in a physical education course to pick up the skills you need for any one of these sports. Physical activity takes your mind off school work and relieves anxiety. There is immediate gratification when you hit that ball, take that stroke, or put in that extra mile. Exercise gets you out of the sack, into the crowd, and reshapes the body. Sound like a wonder drug? It is. Get moving.

SAFETY FIRST

All too often bringing up the subject of using, or not using, a condom comes at the worst time — when no one is thinking too clearly. It may help to have thought beforehand of possible responses if your partner objects to using one, despite the well known health risks involved in unprotected sex.

PARTNER SAYS:	YOU CAN SAY:
"Look, I don't want to talk about this."	"It's difficult for me too, but in my opinion it's best to use one and not be embarrassed."
"Just this once."	"Once is all it takes."
"I don't have one with me."	"I do," or "I don't, so let's satisfy ourselves this time without intercourse."
"I'm really surprised that you have them with you!"	"I have them because I care about myself, and I made sure I had one now because I care about us both."
"My religion is against using birth control devices."	"Then let's hold off until we decide what we really mean to each other."
"I love you. Would I give you an infection?"	"Of course not intentionally. But we can never tell if we are infected. This is best for both of us. It is not meant as an insult."
"Wearing a condom is like taking a shower wearing a raincoat!"	"I've heard that joke before, and it's still pretty silly. We're talking about taking a serious risk."
"If you insist on using a condom I won't have sex with you."	"Since you feel that way, let's put it off until we have a chance to work out our differences."

11. "I'M FROM THE GOVERNMENT AND I'M HERE TO HELP YOU": FINANCIAL AID

A financial aid package is every student's right. Never be too proud to find out what you are due, ashamed that you are "begging," or intimidated by forms or bureaucrats. The applications for grants and loans are going to dog you from the day you enter until you leave, so you might as well get the maximum benefits. Manipulating the facts and figures puts your finances on the right track. Realize there's no such thing as the *correct*, or the *right*, amount due you. You get either *more* or *less*, depending upon how needy you look on paper.

It's in your personal interest to work with your parents (if they are your main support), so that you will know what is going on all through the application process. This saves you from nasty surprises. When you are aware of the limits on your permissible earnings you may not have to pass up the low-paying summer job you really want to help retarded kids, in favor of a heavy-duty construction job. The big bucks might disqualify you, or reduce your grant.

Suppose you decide to go to graduate school and want to declare "financial independence" to qualify for a grant or loan. You won't have a surprise sprung on you that your parents (or one of them) plans to keep taking you as a tax deduction, which might quash your plan.

You are more likely to be aware of filing deadlines than are your parents. The dates differ for the *Financial Aid Form* (*FAF*), administered by the College Board; the *Family Financial Statement* (*FFS*), administered by the American College Testing Program; or the *Application for Federal Student Aid* (AFSA), run by the U.S. Department of Education. Your college or university financial aid office will have its own deadlines. If you live in a state which makes grants, that deadline must be met as well. Submit as early as possible, since the money does run out, especially these days, when the pile is smaller.

What your parents (or you) put on the financial aid form depends heavily upon what is already on income tax returns. The IRS form is the single most important document in the aid process. Information on the IRS return and the financial aid form have to jibe. If your parents (or you) fill out only the short tax form, deductions are being missed that might reduce taxable income to be reported. A reliable accountant is usually worth the fee to fill out a long form. This will pay off later. The less taxable income showing on the tax return, the greater the size of your grant or loan will be.

Some parents delay filing taxes each year. Gently remind them to file early. If you are financially independent, the same goes for eliminating your procrastination. Make duplicate copies of the return to use in the financial aid process.

Filling out financial aid forms is dreary, sometimes intimidating, stuff, but here's a positive view. The folks who administer aid out of Washington (and your state capitol) are not Internal Revenue agents. These mild-mannered officers are giving money away, not taking it in. They have to get rid of all their cash by year's end, or they won't have done their job properly. Help them. So long as you (or your parents) aren't too proud, or too timid, you will get the maximum of what is being handed out.

Here comes the difficult part. If you are not paying your own way through college, your parents are going to have to trust

100

you enough to share some details of their income and expenses. It's better for everyone concerned if this can be done in a relaxed way, since it should be done, like it or not. Obviously, keep this information confidential.

It's never a smart move to knowingly put false or misleading information on your forms, because there are totally legal ways of maximizing grants and loans. Although the divorce or separation of parents is, in all other respects, a sad and unfortunate event, this can have a positive impact by reducing the total available family income which has to be taken into account by the administrators. Exclude the income of either your father (step-father, adoptive father) or mother (step-mother, adoptive mother), depending on the rules. See if you fit the requirements for financial independence or emancipation. This will show up as a big drop in the total income to be taken into account in the calculations.

Do not underestimate the College Work-Study program. Although these jobs usually only pay minimum wage, they are worth more than you think. The income is not taxable, which means that nothing is taken out by withholding. Since the jobs are on campus, there is no transportation cost. Work-study jobs can generally be sandwiched into convenient time slots, so as not to hurt your class or study time.

Keep one file with all your financial aid records. Make a copy of each year's financial aid application so that you (or your parents) can use it as a guide for the following year.

CHECKS AND BALANCES

Too many students are afraid of checkbooks because they have to be "balanced." Actually, it's not hard to do if you start out with the right type of checkbook. The best checks are those that slip into the plastic cover on the side. As you rip out each check, you fill in the side stub left behind. (Avoid checkbooks that rip from the top of the book. They have to be recorded in a separate record keeper. Everybody forgets to make entries.) Not writing the amount, and on what it has been spent, in the side stub each time a check is drawn, is a self-defeating little trick which must be faced up to.

When it comes to balancing your checkbook, any bank manager will be happy to go over the simple procedure, if you don't show up during lunch hour, or after 3:00 p.m. on Friday.

The operation is not complex. When your bank statement arrives, line up all the deposit receipts, machine teller receipts, cancelled checks, and the check book with the stubs. Take the total of all debits (subtractions) which have not yet appeared on the statement, and deduct this from the balance shown on the statement. Next, add to that figure all credits (additions), such as deposits, which do not yet show on the statement. The resulting final figure will tell you exactly how much money is available for you to draw upon for future checks.

12. MANAGING YOUR MONEY

The best way to learn about managing other people's money on the job is to learn to manage your own. This is something to know long before your first big salary comes in ... and goes right out.

Most of us think that budgets are for governments and newlyweds. College students need budgets because they are such receptive markets for advertisers peddling junk food, records, clothes, etc. It's tough to hang on to money in the face of temptations specifically geared to you. Even students with liberal allowances feel immature when they have no control at all over what they spend.

Where to start? An easy way is to collect receipts and checks for a month. List everything you spend in one column. Students living off-campus always have rent, utilities, and food costs. Don't forget "incidentals": movies, records, snacks, drinks, dates, magazines, and auto costs. Try to be as honest as possible, accounting to yourself for every penny.

In a second column, list every source of income. Compare the two columns, and if more is going out than is coming in, look over the spending list again to see where you can cut back. The budget you set up should slightly overestimate expenses and slightly underestimate income, to cover emergencies.

Budgeting takes on a vital importance when you go off the meal plan or leave campus housing. At the end of an un-budgeted month poor management can mean three days of living off popcorn. To make sure you don't starve, at the start of the month buy your basic foods. A household with eggs, tuna, bread, rice, beans, and spaghetti or noodles, will always make it through. Add on weekly purchases of fresh vegetables, fruit, fish, chicken, and the less expensive cuts of red meat. Never set foot in the supermarket without a rough shopping list. Always eat before shopping. Hungry or thirsty people frantically throw expensive junk into the cart.

Be hard nosed about keeping to your estimates. Check over your budget at the end of the first month. Where can you make cuts? After three months of budgeting, your money worries will recede. That's the point of this fussy detail work. *Not* budgeting has only one advantage. You won't blame yourself when you mysteriously run out of money part way through every month.

Still, there may be those dark times when you realize there is no money in the checking account, nothing left in the desk, and the canned goods are gone. Most schools make short-term emergency loans of between $25 to $50 available. Talk with both the bursar and the dean of students about getting one of these short-term loans. A loan, of course, has to be paid back some time, and so must fit into your budget.

102

BUDGET

For month(s): _____

Money in from:

1 _____ $_____
2 _____ _____
3 _____ _____
4 _____ _____
5 _____ _____
6 _____ _____
7 _____ _____
8 _____ _____
9 _____ _____
10 _____ _____

Total in $_____
(Add 1-10)

Money out to:

11 _____ $_____
12 _____ _____
13 _____ _____
14 _____ _____
15 _____ _____
16 _____ _____
17 _____ _____
18 _____ _____
19 _____ _____
20 _____ _____
21 _____ _____
22 _____ _____
23 _____ _____
24 _____ _____
25 _____ _____
26 _____ _____
27 _____ _____
28 _____ _____
29 _____ _____

Total out $_____
(Add 11-29)

From *Total in,*
Subtract *Total out*
Result is *Money Left.*

Money Left $_____

103

13. BILLS, BILLS, BILLS

Managing to live well on your salary after college will be easy enough if you learn to control expenses now.

Telephone bills are big trouble at residential colleges. Two guys from the same high school in Arkansas, who roomed together at an east coast college, spent their first month at school on the phone all day, calling old girlfriends and buddies. When a twenty-two page bill for $800 came in, they started paying attention to the telephone company's discount rates. Signing up for AT&T is an easy way to go, but check out the rates of MCI, US Sprint, or any other long distance service.

Long-distance calls are expensive emotional pacifiers. Look around for local people to lend a sympathetic ear. Friends in college encourage you to stick it out until life improves. The gang at home would like to see you come back.

An automobile is your other biggest single variable expense. Getting along without one, by relying on public transportation or on friends, cuts costs. Commuting students who have to have a car will find that car pooling saves them money on gas, tolls, and parking. As convenient as it is to have a car for yourself, face the costs squarely. Sure, you count the monthly payments in your budget, but don't neglect insurance, gas, and maintenance. Some money is guaranteed to go out for problems that do happen: speeding tickets, parking tickets, and the inevitable repairs.

The one budget buster totally under your control is impulse buying. Eliminating impulse buying is unrealistic. Purchasing things is fun, whether we need them or not, but there are ways of "channeling" impulse buying that reduces the bite. The less cash you carry around, the less you spend.

Bankers have become so friendly, and they have made getting funds so convenient since the advent of the cash card teller machine, that it almost seems unsporting not to take out more than you need. If you do, the surplus is sure to disappear. This is doubly true in the evening, on your way to a good time.

Credit cards also encourage impulse shopping. The interest charges are astronomical, adding as much as 20% to the price per item. Since banks differ in their rates and in their yearly fees, check out every bank in your area to see who offers the best deal. Even better, ask each bank if it issues a "debit" *Visa* or *MasterCard.* This debit card looks exactly like a standard credit card and is accepted everywhere. It draws down on your checking or savings account, at no charge to you (in fact, you will be earning interest on your deposits). Since the debit card is similar to a checkbook, its drawback is that you have to have money in the account ahead of time to cover purchases.

Army surplus stores can save you money, because they offer interesting merchandise at low prices. Another cost saving idea is to shop for vintage clothing and used items, especially appliances. If you want to make a big purchase, and you want it brand new, it's a good idea to hold off long enough to see if you can really live without it. This little stall is pointless if you find yourself deciding every time you just have to have whatever passes through your mind.

14. THE INDOOR TAN: SUMMER AND THE WORKING STUDENT

Ahh, ... summer. Sun-filled days, surfing, a tropical tan. The fondest remembered jobs from high school are usually outdoors: lifeguard, camp counselor, or park attendant. The trouble is that these jobs, if continued on while in college, won't make the best impression on prospective employers.

Students planning to get their careers rolling use summers to try out full-time work. They find the jobs that count towards building a strong resume. Even someone who gets a generous allowance and does not need to work, should establish a record.

Develop a strategy to cover several summers. Go after entry-level jobs in areas related to career interests. Key in the summer before graduation on a job directly related to long-range goals, which are likely to be fairly clear by then.

With a family business backing you up, the path is not complicated since you'll probably be expected to help out. No explanations are necessary on the resume. If the family is agreeable, you should spend the very important summer before graduation somewhere else. Even if you plan to stay with the family business, experience with other firms is valuable.

If you are going to have to end up with a work history loaded with grungy jobs, make it clear in your application letters or interviews that the money from these jobs put you through college. Fortunately, the self-made man or woman still impresses employers.

Look as hard and as long for that right summer spot as for the first real full-time job. Students in the enviable position of having some choice about what they can work at should focus on the summer before graduation. During senior-year interviews this is the job that impresses employers most.

To get a jump on the competition, go to the college placement office in December to talk with them about what firms posted jobs the previous spring. If the office kept the requests, ask to look them over. Contact these firms long before they gear up to send in their new requests, since they will be likely to hire for the spots again and again.

One common path to success is to work at the same place summer after summer. Either you will wrangle a permanent job, or transfer that experience somewhere else.

What follows are some strategies for a few career paths. You should be able to modify these ideas to suit your interests:

Commercial art majors are strong prospects for advertising agencies. Start as a "gofer" or try to get into the infamous mail room, where many a career begins. Then, hook on as an assistant to an artist, using the previous summer's contacts as a starting point.

Getting into health-related services is fairly easy, simply because there are so many facilities. Start out the first summer in a lab (best for those with technical training) or as an orderly in an emergency room. A chemistry or biology major has a good shot at getting something in a research facility. If you show initiative you can upgrade these jobs, summer by summer.

See next chapter.

15. SUMMERS OVERSEAS

Escape the hometown blues by working outside the country. If you are taking a foreign language, a summer job overseas will pay off. In this special case it is location, not position that matters. Be scrupulously honest on your resume concerning these jobs. Learning about native customs and improving your language skills are all that will be important to later employers.

There are jobs, which include room and board, all over the world and in the U.S. at youth hostels. Send for lists to: Y.H.A., National Campus, Delaplane, VA 22025.

Vacations and holidays might mean signing on as an *au pair*, who takes care of children or a household while learning the language and customs of the host family. There are many agencies who place young women. Two are:

England and Overseas
    Au Pair Agency
Suite 29 Kent House
87 Regent Street
London, England WIR 7HF

Relations Internationales
20 Rue de l'Exposition
75007 Paris, France

For unskilled laboring work, check out the London-based international farm camps. Working as a day laborer on a farm means room and board and a little spending money. One of the authors did this not long ago in Switzerland, his summer before junior year. Every morning he woke to see the white-capped Dent-du-Midi mountain range rising in back of shimmering Lake Geneva. Routing out weeds on his knees was not terrific fun, but his French improved significantly when they brought the produce to market.

Place ads for any spot you want in these English language newspapers overseas (write first for rates per insertion):

International Herald Tribune
181 Av. de Charles de'Gaull
Neuilly (Paris) 92521 France
(The *International Herald Tribune* is read throughout Europe)

London Times
Gray's Inn Road
London WC1, England

Rome Daily American
Via Santa Maria, 12
Rome 00187, Italy

Mexico City News
Baleras, 87
Mexico City, Mexico

Japan Times
4-5-4 Shibaura, Minato-ku
Tokyo 108, Japan

Source of information about working outside the country:

Council on Int'l Educ. Exchange
205 E. 42nd Street
New York, NY 10017
212-661-1414

Council on Int'l Educ. Exchange
312 Sutter Street
San Francisco, CA 94108
415-421-3473

16. LANDING INTERNSHIPS

Once you get past your first terms, setting up an internship with a corporation, institution, labor union, or government agency is easy. Getting academic credit for it is only slightly harder. Colleges and universities merely require you to find a willing faculty sponsor and submit a paper or project for grading.

Successful projects are designed, in advance, between the sponsoring professor and the agency or firm. This makes sure that you don't end up answering phones, between bouts of filing mail. In a program one of the authors directed for an inter-departmental urban studies concentration, students placed in internships went on to full-time work in the same location upon graduation.

The program fixed up Brian with a drafting position for a small architectural firm. He designed a first-rate reconstruction of the village square for his three credits. His perseverance and skill impressed the architect so much that she hired him.

Every field has internship possibilities. Retail and fashion trades have business sequences that often coincide with slack periods in the academic schedule. Locate firms that could use an extra, unpaid, hand during the mad buying rushes. The large clothing retailers select their better sportswear and designer items between February and March. The less expensive items are picked out a little later.

TV stations also love that free, star-struck help in the studios.

Instead of finding your own spot, it takes less effort to plug into pre-existing internship programs run by sociology (for social work), political science (for government), and business. Such departments expect students to grab at the opportunity to experience the delights of working in real life situations.

A few colleges go further and integrate paid internships, called co-op programs, into the structure of the curriculum. At Northeastern and Bennington, students go to classes for the first year and then put in tours of co-op duty. More such programs are being made available at various institutions.

One of the authors was lucky enough to stumble upon a paid undergrad internship in New York City with the Mayor's Commission on Taxi Cabs. They gave him a desk, a telephone, and access to a secretary. To justify the confidence, he had to put in the work. At one point he spent some mighty weird weeks, stop watch in hand, at all hours of the day and night, timing how long it took for passengers to get cabs.

Because his part of the task was important, though small, the internship offered him the opportunity to do real work that ended up being incorporated into the official report, as well as receiving a grade.

The *National Directory of Internships*, which may be available at your library, lists over 800 internships and fellowships nationwide. You might also check with the National Society for Internships and Experimental Education, 122 Saint Mary's Street, Raleigh, NC 27605 (Telephone: 919-787-3263).

Good luck.

17. EATING SMART

A college cafeteria is a great place — no exams, no books which have to be read, plenty of company, and, as a bonus, lots and lots and *lots* of food.

A professor friend's first experience with a residential cafeteria came only recently, during a summer he spent at Berkeley. The tray filled magically with two entrees and a mound of potatoes and gravy. A roll, butter, chocolate milk, and a coke with two lemon wedges were add-ons. Back he came for two desserts, coffee, and another glass of chocolate milk. This went on for days. He started falling asleep at his desk afternoons. When he realized that not only was his work suffering, but he was putting on weight, he dropped out of the meal plan.

Most entering students don't have that option. They find other ways around putting on the "freshman 10." To avoid gaining extra pounds, eat three modest-sized meals a day. Sitting down to three meals, even if one is minimal, prevents sudden surges of hunger, and evens out your energy level through the day. This keeps you out of the fast-and-binge cycle. Getting through the line without grabbing everything in sight *is* possible.

Breakfast is the one meal that even cafeteria cooks have trouble ruining. Boiled eggs are healthier than fried, but fried always beat out scrambled, which may be reconstituted from powdered eggs. Fresh fruit is better than orange juice because the natural vitamin D in orange juice has disappeared by the time it's reconstituted. Cut down on sweetened cereals. It's tough to pass up the heavily sugared pastries and donuts — but try. When your blood sugar level shoots up it brings on a major crash in the afternoon. Same lift and crash goes for coffee. Save the jolt from regular coffee for study time.

Lunch is a good time to squeeze the leafy greens in. Hit the salad bar. If lack of time is a problem, think about brown-bagging it with cheese or fresh meat sandwiches on whole wheat bread, plus fruit. Ease up on the soda pop. Carbonated water or club soda gives the same thirst-quenching sensation without all the doubtful ingredients. Save dessert for dinner.

The big rule at dinner is *never* go back for seconds. Watch out for hind leg of dog and turkey tetrachloride, or anything else hidden under a cream or tomato sauce. Fish and chicken rank low in cholesterol, so long as they are not deep fried. Tearing the breading off deep fried foods and slicing the fat from meat keeps your veins from clogging. You can't go wrong with a stripped-down baked potato. Cafeteria cooks put so much salt in everything that the cautious eater will go lightly on the shaker, substituting lemon juice or pepper as a seasoning. Eat slowly at dinner, since no one is going to snatch it away. This aids in digestion and calms you down after a long day.

Fast food is everywhere. For some students it fills in the gaps in the food plan. For other folks, it's the whole shot. Some nutritionists hate the stuff, but others say it's fine. One thing for sure, the all-American trio -- burger, fries, and a chemical shake -- deliver less nutrition for the buck and the bulk than a meat taco, a pizza, or a fried chicken dinner.

See next chapter.

18. COOKING RIGHT

Universities and colleges have strict rules against cooking in unequipped dorm rooms. Set yourself up with food that doesn't need to be heated. Buy or rent a small refrigerator and stock it with juices, milk, cold cuts, yogurt, cheese, salad makings, bread, butter, and mayonnaise. There will probably be just enough room for three flavors of ice cream. Load an empty bookshelf with cups, glasses, knives, forks, spoons, large and small plates, plus bowls. Stack up tuna, salmon, sandwich spreads, peanut butter, cans of beans, olive oil, vinegar, cereal, nuts, raisins, and cookies. Wrap everything tightly or put it in Tupperware. Clean up after eating to avoid sharing your food with uninvited rodents or vermin.

Once the thrill of illegal cooking next to the bed on a hot plate wears off, students tend to move off campus or get into a suite with a kitchen. Face up to the terrors of cooking by getting some information from Mom or by picking up a straightforward manual, like the good old *Fannie Farmer Cookbook.*

Cooking for one is usually a drag. If you share a kitchen with congenial people, set up a weekly meal preparation and cleanup schedule on a rotating basis. One way is for one cook a day to shop for, and prepare, that evening's meal. Another way is to do a communal shop with pooled cash. Communal buying only works if there is secured storage space. Label personal food. One group we knew had two levels. There was personal food you could borrow in a pinch, such as milk or butter. On favorite food that was not to be touched no matter how dire the need — imported beer, Dove Bars, required makings for special diets — they wrote EAD ("Eat And Die"). Divide up the chores, and post a schedule with specified cleanup assignments.

One communal purchase at the start should be a microwave. It's good for plenty more than defrosting frozen food, reheating pizza, or making popcorn. A sack of Idaho potatoes will feed a hungry crowd for weeks.

Cooking isn't always fun, especially on a daily basis, but there's a huge social pay-off for anyone who cooks food that's out of the ordinary. Tackling Mexican, Italian, French, Chinese, or Indian cuisine gives you a great reputation as a host, even if you only know how to prepare one dish. Clean off the table, clear away the boxes, put out a placemat, and sit down. Meal time should serve as a relaxing break in your hectic routine.

Being relaxed and knowledgeable about procedures at mealtime will take you a long way. Confidence at the table has nothing to do with selecting the right fork (start with the implements the furthest out and work in). Hang on through the grungy college years to those good table manners mom taught you. Lunch with prospective employers checking you out won't be a bit nerve wracking.

109

THE START-YOUR-KITCHEN CHECKLIST

Steal as much from home as your mother will let you carry off. Soon you will be able to cook with ease, instead of making macaroni and cheese in the same pot every night.

CHEAP EQUIPMENT:

- ☐ 2 pots (one quart, three quarts)
- ☐ large frying pan (non-stick coated)
- ☐ 2 plastic bowls & tight covers
- ☐ colander (or strainer)
- ☐ spatula
- ☐ 2 *sharp* knives (one long, one short)
- ☐ 2 pot holders (or a glove)
- ☐ can opener
- ☐ casserole dish & cover
- ☐ pitcher
- ☐ mixing bowl
- ☐ big serving spoon
- ☐ large cutting board
- ☐ bottle opener

EXPENSIVE OPTIONS:

- ☐ coffee maker
- ☐ toaster oven
- ☐ microwave oven
- ☐ blender

CLEANERS:

- ☐ liquid dish soap
- ☐ sponges
- ☐ scouring pads
- ☐ scouring powder

WRAPS:

- ☐ aluminum foil
- ☐ clingwrap

STAPLES:

- ☐ sugar (two pound box), salt & pepper, flour (pouring box), cooking oil, olive oil, vinegar, mustard, ketchup, mayonnaise, condensed milk or a box of powdered milk.

SPICES:

- ☐ Italian seasoning, garlic powder, chili powder, paprika, cinnamon, nutmeg, curry powder.

HOT STUFF:

- ☐ cayenne pepper (or tabasco sauce), Mexican salsa

19. ANOREXIA AND BULIMIA

Americans are plagued by eating disorders. Some over-eat, while others compulsively diet. Females are more caught up in these problems than are males.

College women sometimes feel, because of their intelligence, they can control everything in their lives to a greater extent than is possible. They are wrong. Anorexia and bulimia have become virtual fads on campus. Anorexia Nervosa is an extreme rejection of food, which leads to self-starvation. Its symptoms involve an unhealthy weight loss, combined with a bizarre preoccupation with food. Bulimia is the obsessive repeated cycle of binging and purging. This means gorging on enormous amounts of fattening food and then getting rid of it by vomiting or through use of drugs (laxatives or diuretics). It is possible to suffer from both eating disorders at the same time.

According to some psychologists, anorectics typically come from well-off white families that place heavy emphasis on high achievement, perfection, and physical appearance. These families may seem warm and loving on the surface, but actually are unable or unwilling to deal with hidden conflicts. Being over or under recommended weight is an anorectic's way of making a personal statement about accepting or rejecting their family's love.

Another interpretation comes from feminist theorists. Diet is a way to deal with sexual attention. Through manipulation of her body shape an anorectic will strive to be what she considers fashionably slim, thus making her that much more attractive to men. Paradoxically, other anorectics hope to stave off sexuality by eliminating the curves and fat deposits that characterize mature womanhood.

Medical researchers look for a genetic or a biochemical component which makes some people prone to put on weight, eat compulsively, or diet destructively. A sudden surge of weight throws some first-year students into a tail spin (although many women arrive from high school already deeply troubled by eating disorders).

As many as 45% of first-year college women say they would consider bulimia as a way to lose weight. The health hazards are enormous. As for anorectics, if not stopped they can starve themselves to death. This is apparently what happened to the singer Karen Carpenter.

These health problems are not as private as sufferers think. Fellow students notice the rapid weight loss, the deterioration in skin and hair tone, and the growth of hair on the arms of anorectics. Bulimics who live in dorms can't help but leave telltale signs, such as the smell of vomit, and clogged drains.

It's virtually impossible for a roommate to help an anorectic or a bulimic. There is an embarrassed conspiracy of silence that misguidedly protects the sufferer. According to counselors, the problems are too deep-seated to be solved by a friendly talk. Only long-term professional guidance works. Contact a dorm director or call the health service office to get aid for these desperate people. This is not telling on a friend, but rather helping a human being in terrible need.

111

20. AVOIDING DEPRESSION

Students are always being told they "don't know how good they have it," and so shouldn't complain. They stand as much of a chance of being depressed, however, as anyone.

Short periods of sadness and discouragement are natural in college. School is competitive. Everybody wins some and loses some. Doing well academically is no guarantee that everything will be great. Top students put themselves under pressure that can lead to worse mood swings than the average student ever feels.

Anyone can get depressed. Mild depression usually brings on sleeplessness, lowered energy level, loss of appetite, and irritability. It causes free-floating anxiety, feelings of worthlessness, guilt, or self-reproach. The practical result is that you are unable to concentrate on academic work or take pleasure from ordinary things.

It's tough to get a handle on mild depression. Trouble mounts up while no one is looking. No boss is there to complain about your fall-off in performance level. Professors usually do not notice anything about a student's emotional state. Roommates are not parents. They have problems of their own, and will pay as little attention as possible to your moping around.

Depression can be catching, which is why roommates often shield themselves. George was a talented writer with a ready wit who did a biting impersonation of Andy Rooney. When he was in the right mood, he got straight A's. Junior year he was thrown by a break-up with his girlfriend, and a philosophy class where he decided the professor was out to get him. George gave up exercising, went on drinking binges, and cut classes. He lay on his rumpled bed for hours with the door locked. Although he never went over the edge, he developed such a long-standing case of general dissatisfaction that the people he lived with looked the other way, to protect themselves.

When you feel like you are "going crazy" and start to think about looking for help, this is a sure sign you are not "crazy." Really "crazy" people don't ask for help — in fact they passively or actively resist being helped.

To get out of depression, start with your most obvious area of vulnerability — substance abuse. A study of almost 1,000 men between the ages of 21-25, at the University of California at San Diego, revealed that the majority in the most depressed group said alcohol or drug use always preceded their slumps. Before you conclude you are in a hopeless condition, change your recreational habits. Remember alcohol is a depressant and will push you into a downward spiral.

Absolutely don't self-medicate. This means don't borrow your friend's prescription medicine, and despite the TV ads, avoid gulping sleep inducers.

It's not only that too much fun can become no fun at all, but that a heavy social life takes quality time away from your study. Obvious. The guilt and psychological pressure that comes from doing lousy work that leads to poor grades will depress anyone! Get your scheduled study done before you party and you will feel less need to work so hard at having fun.

A SOUND MIND IN A HEALTHY BODY

Alabama football coach, Bear Bryant, justifying athletics at his university: *It's kind of hard to rally 'round a math class.*

* * *

Texas A & M Basketball Coach, Shelby Metcalf, to a player who received four F's and a D: *Son, looks to me like you're spending too much time on one subject.*

* * *

Oklahoma State tackle, Art Flect, on blocking: *I just imagine that the guy on the other side of the line is a professor that's been giving me a bad time.*

* * *

Boston Celtics forward, Marvin Barnes, on why he earned so many college credits while in prison: *There was no place I could go to cut classes.*

* * *

Baltimore disc jockey, Johnny Walker: *The University of Maryland football team members all make straight A's. Their B's are a little crooked.*

* * *

Rice football coach, Al Conover: *I have a master's degree. The subject of my thesis was, "What college done for me."*

* * *

Oklahoma football Coach, Barry Switzer: *It was like a heart transplant. We tried to implant college in him, but his head rejected it.*

* * *

North Carolina-Charlotte basketball coach, Harvey Murphy, when six of his eleven players were ruled academically ineligible: *This is bad for team morale.*

* * *

Miami of Florida football coach, Pete Elliot, on a recruit: *I asked the young man if he was in the top half of his class academically. He said, "No sir, I am one of those who make the top half possible."*

* * *

Texas basketball Coach, Abe Lemons, recalling when two of his players at Oklahoma City University enrolled in a basket-weaving class: *The only problem was that the instructor graded on the curve and there were twenty-four Indians in the class. Both my boys flunked.*

***

113

21. CHASING THE BLUES

Exercise improves emotional well-being. A sports psychologist at Penn State studied two groups of students who reported mild depression. The test group got out and ran daily for eight weeks. The control group did not have a regular exercise schedule. The test group showed a dramatic improvement in overcoming previous sleep problems, fatigue, sadness, withdrawal, and low self-esteem.

Anything that gets the heart pumping will do the same trick. This leaves out checkers and bowling, but includes swimming, cycling and racquet ball. Since women are three times as likely as men to experience depression, they should maintain a regular exercise program. It won't be easy, because they traditionally have had little encouragement to exercise vigorously.

The best way to get started is to go slowly. Any complicated exercise regimen will be a turn-off. It's hard for someone who's already depressed to get moving. A friend can be a great help in motivating you out of the house and into the gym.

No one is sure if the emotional lift in exercise derives from a physiological change in the body, or from the psychological release that comes from concentrating on an activity outside the petty anxieties of your daily routine. People who get into meditation find it works as well as exercise to escape the anxieties of their everyday environment.

There are times when a temporary bout of depression is very natural. A death in the family, or of someone close, is a legitimate cause for grief. Openly express that grief so that it won't burrow underground and emerge disguised in destructive forms.

It's increasingly common for parents to divorce when their youngest child enters college. The loss is traumatic, no matter what happens. The 18-year-old is just as likely to feel the pain as is a toddler. Anticipate a natural period of shock. You will also feel repercussions if your Mother needs surgery, or if your Father is thrown out of work because his company is closing. It's better not to deny the upset to yourself.

These catastrophes throw you off your routine. At least the cause is crystal clear and allowance can be made to admit your human frailty. It's okay to act out, to cry, and to escape from the world. But, if your depression drags on, cannot be shaken, or leads to thoughts of suicide, that's when it's time to ask a professional for help.

Plenty of long-term depressions have a medical cause. Your health service doctor may discover a vitamin deficiency, anemia, a hormonal imbalance, a yeast problem, or the dread mononucleosis. Finding out that your depression has a medical basis goes a long way towards relieving anxiety and puts you on a recovery track.

A long bout of depression leads to diminished interest in your surroundings. Get out of the room and into the open spaces, woods, or streets. Force all your senses to react. It's not a bad idea to stop and smell the roses. Like Bob Marley used to sing: "Lively Up Yourself." Locking the door, lying on the bed, turning up the stereo, and staring at the ceiling day after day, is not the answer.

114

SUICIDE IS NEVER THE ANSWER

YOUR RISK IS HIGHEST:

- Before or after the results are received on an important exam or project.
- When you have just broken up a relationship.
- During the holidays or in the gloom of winter.

Everybody is thrown by a hard time. The crisis *will* pass. Life *will* get better. After a while you will barely remember your present troubles.

WHAT BRINGS ON THOUGHTS OF SUICIDE?

- The fear you "let your parents down." (Let them see you through the transitional period of failure. You are more important to them than your successes or failures.)
- You broke up with the "perfect" person. (It hurts now, but give it time. Love will return. Any campus has plenty of equally great people.)
- You set your aspirations so high failure seems a catastrophe. (Keep plugging. The next time you try something equally worthwhile, you will make it.)

WARNING SIGNS:

- Watch out for sharp mood swings. Be careful not to act on a sudden impulse just after trouble breaks.
- Avoid a bout of heavy drinking to "drown your sorrows." When you are drunk you can't think rationally and the powerful self-protection nature gives us is weakened.
- Don't linger when reading about a well-publicized suicide. Just because someone commits suicide doesn't give you permission to kill yourself.

TO GET THROUGH THIS CRISIS:

- Tell your parents about your feelings right away. They will want to help.
- Call the Suicide Prevention Crisis Counseling Center. The number for your area is in the telephone book, or check with the operator. Let a trained person talk you through this bad time.
- Tell a friend. Don't just drop hints and hope he or she will figure it out in time to save you.

IF A FRIEND TELLS YOU HE OR SHE IS CONSIDERING SUICIDE:

- It's a warning sign if your friend starts giving away his or her possessions, or does far more recreational drugs or alcohol than usual. Take it *very* seriously. Your friend needs help right now — not a day from now.
- Treat a potential suicide as if it were a homicide. There is no privacy or confidentiality to respect. It's not ratting to call their parents or to let an administrator or RA know.

22. SMOKING AND WEIGHT

Companies have been forced to market tobacco to the young because older people are getting out. Since the first Surgeon General's Report in 1964 on the link between smoking and health hazards, per capita consumption has dropped twenty-five percent.

Tobacco companies find that their best pitch is that women should smoke to stay thin. Young females are now the tobacco companies' biggest target. College women are almost twice as likely as college men to smoke every day. This stat comes from a study of 1,100 participants, conducted by the University of Michigan.

June is a typical college woman smoker. She's totally frank about why she smokes. She lost weight at age 16, when she started the habit. Rightly or wrongly, she identifies her Virginia Slims with being thin, even though she also diets. She's up-front about acknowledging that she worries about the health hazards, but that is outdistanced by her terror of putting on any weight whatsoever. She lies about how much she smokes and claims her low-tar cigarettes are safe. She talks about stopping altogether — someday.

The reason June gives for not quitting right away is to keep her weight down. Doctors explain any weight gain that might come after quitting as a consequence of a patient misidentifying the craving for nicotine with hunger pangs. A burst of overeating is the result. Learn to recognize the difference between your intense desire for a cigarette and the entirely different desire of mental confusion about what the body actually wants.

When your need for nicotine diminishes, your misidentification with hunger pangs will disappear. You'll soon stop feeling hungry. Realistically, during the nicotine withdrawal period experts predict an increase of perhaps three to five pounds. We should hold it, right here. Some of our readers might make the decision not to quit because gaining even a pound induces panic. According to our conversation with Doctor Michael Cummins at a world-famous cancer research center, Roswell Park Memorial Institute, most of this poundage is a *temporary* increase in water weight entirely due to hormonal changes.

When they quit smoking, both men and women undergo a change in their metabolism, that is, the rate at which their bodies burn calories. Since nicotine is a stimulant, it forced the pace at which food was utilized. After dropping cigarettes, your body will put out the same amount of energy *with far less food intake*.

So, the way to quit smoking while maintaining your basic weight is to consume fewer calories than before. This won't be hard for anyone who has ever dieted. A doctor, or an expert on nutrition, can prescribe the proper diet and recommend suitable exercises to keep any temporary weight gain to a minimum. Constant monitoring of weight, and some positive reinforcement from friends, gets a person through the nicotine fits and the Twinkie binges. Sure, it's going to be tough, but it will be worth it.

23. THE WARNING ON THE PACK

The tobacco industry links smoking with glamour and gets away with it! Amazing! Think about the bad breath, the yellow teeth, and the ever-present smell.

That's all superficial and gets masked by toothpaste and perfumes. You can't do anything about repairing what doctors call "smoker's face." Nicotine restricts blood flow to the extremities, which include the face. With less blood nurturing the cells, the skin on the face ages rapidly. It doesn't take many years of smoking to get pucker lines around your mouth from puffing. Squinting through smoke causes crowsfeet around your eyes. Put this way, smoking sounds pretty nasty. And don't forget cancer.

Someone is always sure to say that since everything causes cancer they'll choose their poison. Not true: (A) Not everything causes cancer; (B) Tobacco sure does. Lung cancer kills 38,600 women a year. Let's repeat that: 38,600 individual women are dead now because they smoked. According to the American Cancer Society, five times as many women died in 1986 from lung cancer than did 20 years before, purely a result of increased smoking.

Using smokeless tobacco isn't a safe way out. The industry tells young men that its product doesn't cut down on wind as much as cigarettes. True enough, but plenty of cases of mouth cancer are coming to the attention of doctors.

Certain campuses smell like chimneys because they hang on to the tradition that smoking is a prompt for conversation and a sop for tension. On a campus like this, consumption will double during finals week. Students haul out the cigs whenever they pull an all-nighter. Just don't go cold turkey during such high tension periods. Quitting is easiest at the start of a term, or after finals.

There are many ways to reduce the tensions of college life, besides smoking. Being prepared and knowing how to handle the work is much more effective than any number of cancer sticks.

Non-smoking is the wave of the future, anyway. The right to smoke is everywhere on the decline. The shorter the time you have smoked, the easier it is to get out from under. Few people entering college will have put in many years. In the eighteen to twenty-five age group nationally, only fourteen percent of college students smoke every day. This is small compared to the twenty-four percent of smokers in the same age group who have not gone on to college. The body has superb recuperative powers. Damage done to your lungs, heart, and other organs is repaired with astonishing speed, as soon as you quit. The younger you are, the easier it is to escape this dangerous habit.

24. ALCOHOL: THE CAMPUS "DRUG OF CHOICE"

How can we talk about drinking without turning you off? If you want to avoid the topic, just rip out these pages and throw them away.

It's no surprise that plenty of drinking goes on, although not everyone does it. In a University of Michigan nation-wide study, 57% of college students said they had a drink within the previous thirty days.

Some of these students drink considerably more than others, though. Men consistently knock down more than do women. Guys under twenty-one put away plenty when they drink, and do it faster than anyone else.

Because colleges and party bars are proofing much more carefully now, "front loading," that high school trick of having a few quick ones at home before hitting a party, is getting popular again. An assistant dean at the University of Vermont sees it this way: "Students are going to drink, regardless of where, when, or how."

Lower classmen — who are at greatest risk of messing up their college careers — need to cut back on heavy drinking bouts. Learn from upperclassmen, who stretch out their drinking and consume less when they go out for the evening. The drinking pattern displayed by these older students has been charted in a study of more than 3,000 undergrads enrolled in the University of California-Berkeley, and at Davis. Older male students go out for a drink more often during the week than do freshmen, but they rarely down more than two or three drinks at a setting. They have learned to drink smart.

Here are some hints on how to avoid wasting the whole next day with a hangover, save some cash, and miss out on a DWI. Eat before going out. A few slices of pizza will slow down your stomach's alcohol absorption rate. If you don't have time to eat something starchy, a quick glass of milk will provide a protective barrier in the stomach.

Reduce consumption by an alternation between glasses of alcoholic and non-alcoholic beverages. A glass of orange juice or cola easily masquerades as a screwdriver or a rum and coke.

When you are at the kind of party where you can mix your own drinks, don't make someone else responsible for the amount of alcohol being poured into your glass. If there is a bartender, ask for a light one. Sip, don't gulp, so time between ordering can be stretched out. Alcohol hits the bloodstream fast when the mixer is carbonated, which means scotch and soda enters the system quicker than a scotch and water.

The college drinker's first choice is, has, and always will be, that golden elixir brewed from the finest spring water, malt, and hops. It's easy to underestimate its impact. A draft beer has as much alcohol as a standard shot of distilled spirits.

When the brew comes in a keg or pitcher, drinking moderately becomes a challenge. Get up from the table now and then. Not only does taking a walk clear your head, but it's a sure-fire way to miss a couple of rounds. Let a full glass of beer stand. No one will notice.

Chugging contests and shotgunning should probably be avoided.

25. TOO MUCH, TOO OFTEN: LOSING CONTROL OF DRINKING

For some, no evening's entertainment is complete without a final stop at the bathroom to puke and pass out. Almost half of college students surveyed by the University of Michigan admitted to occasionally downing five or more drinks in a row. Being the first in your dorm to suck down an entire bowl of Mad Dog Scorpion Punch, or other weirdly named mixture of Kool-Aid and grain alcohol at the Tropical Marathon Party is not always a worthy ambition.

Jane Jacobs, the prominent author, asked us to include her story here. She had never had a drink in her life when she showed up on campus. On a dare, she chugged a bottle of Jack Daniels. Halfway through, she passed out. Her terrified companions called an ambulance. The attending physician pumped her stomach just in time to save her. He had seen cases where even less neutral spirits, taken in a gulp, had killed kids.

Students who drink occasionally do well enough in class; few who consistently drink too much can say the same. Five percent of college students drink every day. They are slipping over that line that separates the alcohol abuser from the alcoholic. If you find yourself getting drunk when you don't want to — when it's the worst possible time to get drunk or when it could be downright disastrous — then your drinking can't be called ordinary. The grades slip, then you drink to feel better. Getting up later and later every morning, with a hangover, is a key warning sign of trouble. Reorientation into becoming a night owl means your assignments get done at 2:00 a.m., if they get done at all.

Ten percent of the drinkers in America down half the booze. Defining oneself as an alcoholic is something people with the problem avoid. As the Welsh poet Dylan Thomas (who died of drink at 39) said, "An alcoholic is someone you don't like who drinks as well as you do." Alcoholics lose their ability to predict how much they will drink, they begin to blackout, and they drink in the morning to recover.

Alcoholics can never discipline themselves to become "social drinkers" because they're victims of a kind of disease or genetic program malfunction. Recognize that there is a problem and then get help. It's hard for anyone to dry out on their own. College administrators are well aware of alcoholism and can offer help. Talk things out with a sympathetic RA, a counselor, or the personnel at the college clinic.

It's impossible to mention drinking without bringing up driving. Hard drinkers learn to modify their driving under the influence, at least for a while. Folks new to drinking rely upon a burst of "Dutch courage" to get away with high speed or a bit of tricky driving. One time that margin will be too thin. Over 50,000 young people are killed or disfigured annually. Even minor crack-ups where no one is hurt mean expensive auto repair bills. In a way, anyone who loves their car shouldn't drink and drive.

The drinking age has been going up to protect society from young drunk drivers, and drivers from themselves. College students are far less selfish on this question than most of the outside world thinks. In the University of Michigan study mentioned earlier, two-thirds of the respondents thought that every state should raise its drinking age to 21.

PROBLEM CASE — ANYONE YOU KNOW?

It's really hard to admit that a friend or roommate has a problem. People slipping into trouble with alcohol or drugs are practiced at hiding the problem from themselves and others.

Answer these questions as honestly as possible. If you are the one with the problem you have nothing to lose and a lot to gain by going through the list.

Check all of the statements that are true.

- ☐ Have a parent who is alcoholic?
- ☐ Miss morning classes because of drinking the night before?
- ☐ Made uncomfortable by subject of drug abuse or alcoholism?
- ☐ Gotten angry when confronted with evidence of abuse?
- ☐ Feel uncomfortable in social situations when alcohol is not served?
- ☐ Partying always means drinks or drugs?
- ☐ Drink alone or try to conceal drinking?
- ☐ Regret things said when drinking?
- ☐ Change friends to accommodate habits?
- ☐ Switch from one type of drink to another to control drinking?
- ☐ Avoid friends or family when drinking?
- ☐ Complain of weight loss, sleeplessness, low energy, inefficiency, or accidents related to drinking?
- ☐ Get drunk more quickly with less alcohol?
- ☐ Can't really have a problem because only "bums" lying in the gutter are alcoholics?
- ☐ Buy liquor at different places to conceal extent of drinking?
- ☐ Drink to "relieve tension?"
- ☐ Always saying it's not hard to quit any time?
- ☐ Did badly on more than one test because of a hangover?
- ☐ Get into fights and accidents related to drinking or drugs?
- ☐ Wish people would mind their own business when it comes to alcohol or drugs?

If you checked more than one of these questions, the person you're concerned about may have a problem that requires help. This person (or yourself) may not be addicted, but could have the potential for a serious problem. Help is needed now. Today would be a good time to make an appointment with a professional counselor with alcohol and drug abuse training. Getting involved shows you care.

These questions are based on material from the Michigan Alcoholism Screening Test, Alcoholics Anonymous, Al-Anon, and the National Council on Alcoholism.

26. MARIJUANA

Public opinion hangs on to the notion that college is still the home base of the drug culture. That's an outmoded stereotype. Students smoke, snort, swallow, and shoot considerably less, on the average, than others in their age group who do not go to college. Sure, drugs may be present on your campus, but use has gone down all through the 1980's. According to a massive ten-year study conducted by the University of Michigan, use of tranquilizers, barbiturates, amphetamines, methaqualone, LSD and, believe it or not, marijuana, has steadily decreased.

Marijuana (cannabis, pot, grass, joints, and ganga) remains the most prevalent drug on campus, after alcohol. From the start to the middle of the 1980's use dropped from 51% to 42% of the student body, but it's still passed around at plenty of social occasions. As with alcohol, the rule is not to indulge just to please others. Even though use has declined, it's always worth learning what "controlled substances" do to the body and how they affect class work.

After years of medical study, definite conclusions are finally available about marijuana. Heavy smoking of joints is now known to bring on sinusitis, bronchitis, asthma, and other breathing disorders far more quickly than will heavy smoking of cigarettes. Aspergillus fungus infections are another problem. This fungus, which is like the stuff found in damp basements, grows on the bales when they are smuggled in via damp, wet shipholds. When smoked, the microscopic fungus floats into the tiny branches of the lungs where it impairs breathing.

One sufferer was described by a University of Wisconsin study as being a "walking fungus ball, with the stuff growing on his lungs, kidneys, skin, and nose."

Scientific studies show that marijuana has a negative impact on memory. A University of Kentucky Medical Center experiment found that users could not recall as many words on a list as could non-smokers. At a minimum, avoid smoking right before exams. If you smoke late at night, it is likely you'll wake up disoriented and tired. It's unclear how bad the long-term memory impact will be for the 3% who smoke every day, but it seems chancy to gamble. Consistent solitary use is, at the least, a sign that someone has dropped out of society.

The biggest gamble of all is guessing what's actually in the little bag. Grass can be laced with all kinds of nasty chemicals. What you see is not necessarily what you get.

27. COCAINE

Cocaine (coke, toot, snow, blow) once had glamour. It was taken up by media and sports stars, along with hard-driving business types. Cocaine became an important part of the late night life style, where the point is to keep going with the use of anything that will do the job. The glamour of nose bleeds and reconstructive facial surgery has now been democratized.

The entrepreneurial drug culture now makes cocaine and crack available to anyone who wants it. Unfortunately, there's no way of telling what's in the white powder, which can be cut with anything inventive from talc to baby laxative.

What about campus use? Dr. Lloyd D. Johnson, director of a University of Michigan study, said, "Students report cocaine to be fairly readily available and, until very recently at least, the great majority saw little risk in experimenting with it." Even so, only 17% of students surveyed have ever tried the stuff, even once.

Researchers are scrambling to find out what it does to the body. The Bronx Veterans Administration Medical Center sounded the alarm. The purity of cocaine available on the street has been increasing, with devastating impact upon the first-time user.

Sudden deaths have been reported, either through sniffing, injection, or being smoked in a crack or free base form. Why? Cocaine over-sensitizes the heart to the normal stimulant effect of the body's adrenaline. With a sudden surge in pressure, blood vessels break or the heart muscle itself undergoes coronary spasm, producing a heart attack. A number of college and pro athletes have died in just this way, so being in top physical shape doesn't make any difference.

College administrators come down hard because drugs bring trouble. Hiding a cache of drugs or a stack of bills in a dorm invites rip-offs. Sellers get into hassles with their suppliers, who can be very rough indeed. Students who sell to their classmates put themselves at risk of expulsion, arrest, or worse.

Cocaine use can bring on paranoia and Benton had good reasons to be on the run. He did all the drugs he could find in prep school, but specialized in cocaine at college. It didn't take him long to get into dealing, even though his profits went up his nose. He enjoyed the notoriety and a sense of being outside the law. Plenty of cash meant throwing big parties and being popular.

When he fell behind in payments to his suppliers, a couple of ill-shaven guys in European-cut suits started shadowing his room. He hid out with his girlfriend at her apartment. Rumors that an FBI-DEA Task Force had targeted his suppliers increased Benton's anxiety, which was already strong from the coke he took. He wouldn't answer the phone and never responded to knocks. When he realized that the college administration had heard about him from the federal agents, he withdrew to avoid disciplinary proceedings. When last seen, he was talking about cutting back.

If you have to be told not to experiment, even once, with crack, you must have been on the moon the last few years.

28. CONTROLLED SUBSTANCES III

Students take amphetamines (speed, bennies, uppers, and pep pills) when they have exams or papers. They're hoping that staying awake for four straight days will make up for work they should have put in earlier. Sometimes it does, but the consequences are rough.

The burst of alertness and efficiency will be followed by drowsiness. The warning signs are increasing agitation and irritability. Amphetamines override the body's protective devices. Speed greatly reduces appetite, so when users come off their "jags" they are tired because their bodies have run out of fuel. Users grossly overdraw their energy account, which can lead to a total collapse if pushed too far.

One out of nine college students used amphetamines at least once during the year, according to a University of Michigan study. Students who rely on amphetamines to get them through heavy work loads are making a mistake. Speed gives only an illusion of increased competence, not the reality that comes from systematic study. What happens over and over again is that students smother fatigue with amphetamines but show up on the big day a total wreck. The grades turn out to be lousy.

Amphetamine abusers turn to barbiturates (downers) and tranquilizers to come down from their jags. Elvis Presley died from this combination. Since barbiturates and methaqualone (ludes) are not common on campus, this saves students from the lethal drug and alcohol combination. Mixing booze and barbiturates killed Marilyn Monroe. If you are on any prescribed or over-the-counter medications (such as antihistamines, anti-diabetic agents, antibiotics, sedatives, or diuretics) avoid liquor, just to be safe.

A whole range of substance abuse hardly shows up at all on the campus: heroin addiction, glue sniffing, taking angel dust (PCP), or swallowing "designer drugs" (synthetic opiates). Even though few students are involved, these substances may be causing one of your friends pain right now.

Anyone who knows a sufferer (or is caught themselves) should go to the college infirmary or contact a doctor. Call the PRIDE Drug Information Line (1-800-677-7433) during the day for referrals, or after 5:00 PM for various tapes.

Timothy Leary and Carlos Castaneda, the drug gurus of the 60's, promoted LSD, peyote and magic mushrooms as liberating portals to other-worldly wisdom. Students just don't buy that pseudo-spiritual angle any more. Only 2% of students experiment with LSD. Just as well. The campus burn-outs and walking wounded from the old days are still hanging out on the fringes of university districts.

There's one mind-altering drug which we recommend wholeheartedly: phenylethylamine (PEA). This is a wonderful substance, produced naturally by the brain when people are happy or in love.

PEA is found in highest concentration in a compound that comes in blocks, is cut with sugar, rarely costs more than $20 a pound, and is dark brown in color. Its street name is chocolate. In modest amounts, it's good for what ails you.

SOME HEALTH QUESTIONS
ONLY YOU CAN ANSWER

If things are not going that great and you don't feel terrific, why not visit the clinic now or see your doctor when you get home on break?

Answer these questions first so that you might have more to talk about in your consultation time.

What concerns me most about my health is...

I take the following prescription and non-prescription drugs...

During the school week, I sleep...

On weekends, I normally sleep...

The truth about what I eat is...

The aspect of my diet I would most like to change is...

Because of my eating habits, I...

The last time I had any serious exercise was...

The way I usually exercise is...

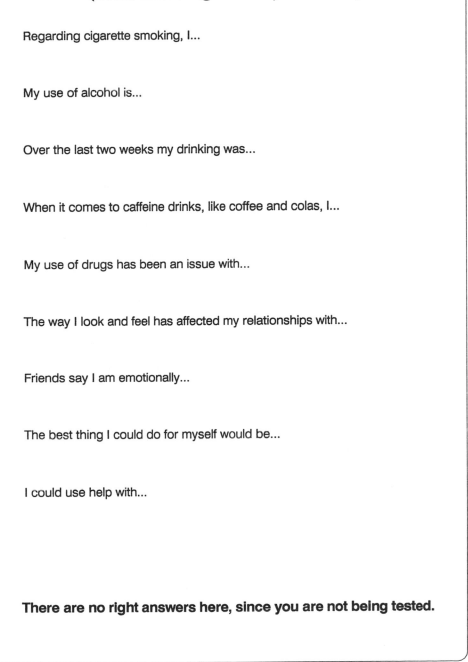

(Some Health Questions, continued)

Regarding cigarette smoking, I...

My use of alcohol is...

Over the last two weeks my drinking was...

When it comes to caffeine drinks, like coffee and colas, I...

My use of drugs has been an issue with...

The way I look and feel has affected my relationships with...

Friends say I am emotionally...

The best thing I could do for myself would be...

I could use help with...

There are no right answers here, since you are not being tested.

29. THE COMMUTING GRIND

Every once in a while a friend of ours gets nostalgic for the college life he never had — dorms, pep rallies, tweedy professors strolling through the quad, and an autumn carpet of red leaves under foot. What never makes it into this fantasy are the cars prowling the parking lots desperate for a space, and an anxious crowd waiting for the last bus of the evening.

A little realism never hurts. Far more people live off campus than on, and part-timers outnumber full-timers 3 to 1, nationally. It's tough being a commuter. There are the hassles of getting back and forth, while being partly in and partly out of the social scene.

Unfortunately, commuters who live at home with their parents have to prove their commitment to college work all the time. Commuters don't get out of family obligations if it looks to others as if they are "wasting time." Watching the tube, languishing in the bath tub, or cruising around with neighborhood friends may not hold you back in your classes, but it looks bad to the rest of the family. To avoid being hassled, keep out of the way, with your nose in a book. Calmly discuss your new needs with everybody, putting the focus upon the difficulties of college-level work. Hanging a sign on your door saying "Student at Work" is a sure way to incite hostility.

A married commuter deserves understanding. Communication with your spouse is vital to ease up on suspicions and jealousies caused by one person having to go away to school so often. Bring your spouse to campus once in a while. This makes the place which consumes so much of your attention less threatening. Married students make the mistake, out of guilt, of rushing home immediately after class. They never allow themselves to meet other students or to get to know their profs.

The authors of this book can offer insight from both sides of the fence on this question. Prof. Lunenfeld still remembers how much he hated spending Saturdays and Sundays in the library, when he wanted to be out in the park with his family. Peter maintains it wasn't as bad as all that, because his father gave him more time than he now recalls. There are only two things out of the ordinary Peter remembers about growing up with a part-time grad student for a father. One was that there were file card boxes and papers lying all around the house that he wasn't supposed to touch, and the other was that he remembers being very proud, as a six-year old, at his father's graduation, without quite knowing why.

See next chapter.

30. EASING THE COMMUTE

Parking is a major problem on *every* campus. People cut their time too tight and arrive at classes or exams angry and frustrated. Set out fifteen minutes early to cut down on your psychological wear and tear.

Being all alone in a car is virtually a constitutional right, but car pooling makes special sense for students. While somebody else does the driving, you get a last minute chance to prepare, or to sleep. Being dropped off can save you precious minutes the day of your exam. See if there is a ride board. If not, run off some tear sheets with your phone number and post these in classrooms.

Pooling has a disadvantage. If any one rider is chronically late, it gets everybody angry. Setting a time when the car will leave, with or without others, avoids arguments.

No matter how commuters get to their college, once they arrive they deserve the same fair treatment as residential students. Don't let any teacher or bureaucrat be contemptuous, or shunt your problems aside. Professors shouldn't consistently run classes overtime, especially at night. Tell your professor that this is hard on everybody. If your professor doesn't change, quietly pick up and go.

You shouldn't get penalized for standing up for your right to leave for home at a reasonable time. Your dean will back you up on this.

Commuters too often cut themselves out of any participation in the academic community. The temptation is terrifically strong to go home as soon as your class is over. If you are a night student you will probably be exhausted by the time the prof stops talking. It's selling the college experience short to shove your books in the bag and take off, though. Talk with some sympathetic fellow students about getting together for coffee after class.

Use the time while trapped on a moving public vehicle to meet new people. All it takes is a little courage to start up a conversation, but there's nothing easier than talking about bus schedules, how hot the train is, or how courses are going.

Sometimes the only way to have any contact is to join a group. Consider pledging a fraternity or sorority. Glee clubs or professional societies offer friendships to older students. Even if it seems impossible to find a single extra free hour in the week, you have to do this so that you don't think of college as only a burden, and nothing more than that.

31. THE MATURE STUDENT: OLDER AND WISER

The first term is always the toughest for mature students. You fear that you won't be up to the work. Your writing skills are creaky. The vocabulary in the classroom is unfamiliar. Exams come all at once. Professors talk too fast. These are real problems, but once school becomes routine, they solve themselves.

Scientific studies show that the mind remains capable and flexible into old age, so fears that your memory is getting worse and that you won't remember as much as you once did are nonsense. In any case, everyone tends to exaggerate how little they remember. Older persons who keep records and notes are more on top of things than younger students, who are cocky about holding data in their heads.

A mother-daughter team took Introductory Biology. They sat in the front row. Mrs. Green took extensive notes, but her daughter, Sarah, did not. She relied on Mom, since they reviewed together. Mrs. Green got an A on every exam, handed her papers in on time, and always asked questions. Sarah was quiet, missed a number of sessions, and gave in slipshod work. Mrs. Green earned her A, but Sarah settled for a C. The professor would ask Mrs. Green what was up with Sarah and she would shrug, saying her daughter was just too young to appreciate the value of education.

Mrs. Green is like other highly motivated older students we know. They feel there is no room for not taking everything down because college is their big chance, arrived at after great sacrifice. It's okay to loosen up. College does accommodate itself to less than ideal work.

Older people worry needlessly they have nothing in common with younger students. In the opening to Marilyn French's *The Women's Room* a returning older student cowers in a washroom stall the first day of class. She will not unlock the door to mix with the stream of students because she feels out of place. Yet, by the end of the novel she has become totally competent. The reality is that younger students are so self-centered they hardly notice mature persons, much less think them out of place. A student is a student is a student.

Even with their string of degrees, professors are approachable. Most teachers are driven crazy by dealing with no one but kids, and like to see a little gray hair once in a while. Returnees always have something going for them. They have varied experiences, and a living memory that goes back more than just ten years.

Older students are the college administrators hottest market, since there's been a 20% fall-off in the 18- to 22-year age group. Administrators are in an older person's corner and will always help you out.

We are all more flexible than we think. At first, returnees wear clothes like protective suits of armor. Women stick to fussy dresses and men arrive in jacket and tie. Relax. You will soon feel comfortable dressing less formally. It doesn't take long to blend in.

See next chapter.

128

32. INTELLECTUAL ADVENTURE IS NOT JUST FOR KIDS

Mature individuals going after their degrees generally focus intently on vocational goals. After all, school is expensive and time consuming.

When women allow themselves the "luxury" of going to college, they worry that they are neglecting their families. Often, their husbands find it hard to adjust to not having their wives around all the time, or out working. Children sure know how to make things tough for Mom when she creates a space in her life that excludes them.

Counselors tell us that the best time to head-off problems with the family is right at the start. Sit everyone down and tell them the house isn't going to be entirely one person's responsibility anymore. The floors won't be clean enough to eat off, but with the right attitude on everybody's part this will not make a bit of difference. There may be some sabotage at first, so expect this and don't be so crushed that you consider dropping out of school.

Whatever their career goals, men and women should think about taking a few interesting, non-vocational, courses to ease up on the grind. College can be an intellectual adventure, one that it would be a shame to totally miss. This keeps you in school when the going gets rough or the job-related courses prove totally boring. It takes a bit of courage for goal-directed persons to sign up for a course on a subject which has always interested them, such as Great Books, psychology, or beginning piano.

It is only then that you begin to find out what *really* interests you. A community

college fine art instructor recalls Louise, an overworked woman with crooked teeth, seven children, and a demanding husband. To pay her way through school, Louise worked an early morning shift at a diner. She was practical and took bookkeeping so that she could get work in a small office. One day she wandered into the pottery studio. That started Louise off taking a broad range of courses that interested her, including English.

This turn of events confused her husband, who thought she was just in college to improve the family's earnings. After a good many discussions and arguments, he came to agree she was doing the right thing. The courses pointed Louise towards teaching. Her art instructor now occasionally sees her former student, well groomed in a classic suit, her teeth straightened, stuffed briefcase in hand, on her way to teach English classes at the same college from which she received her first degree.

Think about financing college by working at the institution itself. Employees usually save either by a tuition waiver or a partial rebate. A tuition waiver plus salary makes a low-paying college job attractive. This way, you will feel more connected with the school.

Older students have a great deal going for them. They know all too well what the "real world" is like. The alternate world of college, with all its varied intellectual and emotional stimulations, holds tremendous interest. They're sure less likely to be diverted from studies by goofing off.

33. MAINTAINING YOUR ETHNIC AND CULTURAL IDENTITY

"Upward mobility," is a very popular phrase in America which seems to offer only promise. Moving from one social level to another really means fitting into the majority community, and internalizing its values and attitudes. This can lead to plenty of pain, because colleges and universities generally do not appreciate the unique and powerful heritages of their ethnic and religious minorities. The leaders of these institutions believe they have a mission to erase differences, so that a standardized product will be turned out. First-year students are asked to reject what they were. This piles social stress on an already tough financial and academic adjustment.

You can prepare yourself, right from the start, to head off the inevitable symptoms of this stressful move towards fitting in: withdrawal, depression, procrastination, and rage. The more you know about your culture, the less reason you have totally to buy in to assimilation, and the easier it will be to protect yourself from anguish. If there is a course on your culture, take it as soon as possible. If not, read up on the history of your people. Experts recommend buying books by authors who come from your background to build up a small library you can share with friends. Start collecting records.

Even under the best circumstances, defending your heritage, combined with all the typical academic tensions, can cause you problems. Don't wait until a crisis arises to begin learning how to manage. Proper diet and enough sleep are vital. Cut down on stimulants and begin to practice relaxation techniques. Above all, talk your anxieties out with as many people from your background as possible. Join an affinity group with similar interests.

Financial problems cause stress like nothing else. Getting into college is a milestone, but it's only one step on your long, long road to the degree. Sometimes grant money or financial aid is suddenly reduced, or an athletic scholarship will not be renewed.

These financial incentives are intended to help you go to school, but must not become the primary reason you attend. As disastrous as it may be if the money becomes tight, this will not be as big a catastrophe as never graduating. Regroup, and take a couple of courses a term, if need be, to stay with it until the end.

Watch out for traps along the way. Where you sit in a classroom can show how you think you are going to do. A study of college students' seating choices in the District of Columbia showed that a definite pattern was established. White Anglo-Saxon Protestants tended to sit in the central seats of the classroom in greater proportions than Catholics, Jews, and those with foreign-born parents.

Ethnic and religious minority students came to class early so that they could remain "outsiders" by choosing the seats in the back and on the outside. It's easy to avoid falling into this pattern. The prime seats are up front and center. Sitting there means you are making a conscious effort to succeed.

RIGHTS OF THE STUDENT WHO IS HANDICAPPED

Public Law (PL) 94-142 provides for a free, appropriate public education for all students, between the ages of three and twenty-one, who are disabled. It is permanent legislation, with no expiration date. The law says that individualized educational programs must be developed for each covered person, and reviewed every year. To the maximum extent appropriate, special students should be educated with the nondisabled, but if you and your parents don't think that will work for you, you don't have to be mainstreamed. These legal changes are hard for many parents to believe, since they have lived for so long with the old attitudes of discrimination. You can help educate them about your rights. The school must instruct and test in the mode that you use. You can select braille, American Sign Language (ASL), a recorder, or whatever you need.

It's your right to make your own decisions, although all too often parents, counselors or schools act as if they were entirely responsible for you. Sometimes, when you want a course, your advisor will tell you that you are not being realistic, because your disability will hold you back. This may turn out to be true, but you, like all students, should be allowed to try and fail or succeed on your own.

Before you set out for a campus, investigate the resources it makes available for special students. Ask to speak to the advocates for the handicapped and, especially, a counselor. Get the name of an enrolled student with a problem similar to yours, so that you can call and see how thoroughly promises are carried out. You need a counselor who will fight for your interests, since it's tough to struggle all alone. If you require a van and your driver turns out to be abusive or strands you, your counselor has to go to bat for you. Sometimes you will be told you can't ever drive an automobile, but investigate specially designed, hand-operated controls anyway. The point, according to Joyce Slayton Mitchell, in *See Me More Clearly*, is to minimize your disability and maximize your abilities. By not concentrating upon your physical differences, you center, instead, on your likenesses with others.

The Americans With Disabilities Act, passed in 1990, simplifies the enforcement procedure for discrimination based on employment. In case this applies to you, individuals who believe they have suffered such discrimination will have the right to file a complaint with the Equal Employment Opportunity Commission. An employer now has an affirmative duty to make responsible accommodation for the physical or mental limitations of an otherwise qualified individual with a disability.

Your legal rights are spelled out in a free government pamphlet, *Handicapped Person's Rights Under Federal Law*. The publication explains federal rules affecting the handicapped that colleges and universities must follow. It's useful to have this publication at hand when dealing with an administration which might not be willing to provide you with an interpreter or signer, or which delays on working towards wheelchair access.

Write: Office for Civil Rights, Department of Education, 330 C. Street, S.W., Washington, D.C. 20202.

34. TO THE BLACK STUDENT

By Paul Ruffins
with historical research by Fath Davis Ruffins.

Black students, here's a little advice from your older brothers and sisters. As two Afro-Americans who really enjoyed the opportunity to get a fine education, we want all black students to have a successful and enjoyable college experience. So, during our 15th reunion we went back to Harvard and asked black administrators and alumni what advice they would give to black students on campuses across the country. Here's their advice on coping with racism and the other stresses of going to school in the 1990s.

Argue historically, not individually.

"Remember the history of how this whole situation came about," advises Marcia Turner, a Ph.D. who is back on campus on an administrative fellowship. Current strategies to increase minority students were developed to rectify a long historical situation in which whites reserved certain advantages for themselves. In response to the civil rights movement, affirmative action was developed as a just alternative to, for example, financial reparations to blacks for past injustices.

The question: "Why is it fair that they chose a black student over a similar white student?" is like the question "Why is it fair that I can't deduct my rent, but you can deduct your mortgage interest?" The answer is that public policies that seek to promote certain social goods, like home ownership, or increasing black college grads, can justly favor some individuals over others.

Know why colleges and universities admit whom they admit.

David L. Evans, a black, Senior Admissions Officer, explains that few, if any, universities simply admit the applicants with the best grades and highest SAT scores. If so, colleges wouldn't require interviews, essays, or recommendations. Evans feels that if more white students understood how they were admitted, they might be less resentful. White students, at least at Harvard, wildly overestimate the number of black and Asian students on campus. Evans states that "Harvard gets eight qualified applicants for every one we accept, so if we took no black students, there would still be 8,000 who didn't get in and think it was the 100 to 150 black students that kept them out, even though the black students were also presidents of their schools, or captains of the debating team."

He adds, "Ninety percent of all students admitted to Harvard and other fine schools get in for reasons other than academic excellence alone. We could fill the class twice with students with perfect records. However, that means we would never have any athletes, or music majors, or plays on campus. But once they're here you can't tell which students got in because they grew up on a farm. But people think they can see who got in because they're black."

Resist the notion that you are "unqualified."

Don't let anyone presume that all or even most black students have poor academic credentials or are all on scholarships. Patricia Rhymer-Todman, who has a Ph.D. in psychology says, "Nobody who is knowledgeable thinks that SATs predict anything in the real world, except how middle-class students do in the first year of college. When people make an issue of the fact that some minority students are admitted with lower scores, they never say whether those differences are statistically significant."

Calibrate your responses to racism.

All racial incidents are not the same and neither should be your response. If someone attacks you publicly, do some research, and engage in debate. In the early 1970s a black Harvard professor named Martin Kilson wrote a widely publicized article charging that black students practiced segregation by always sitting together in the cafeterias. In response, a group of black students conducted research which found that while many black students did sit together, most had a wider range of friends and were involved in a greater variety of activities than most white students. This research was far more effective than picketing or branding Kilson an Uncle Tom.

Be aware of the role of colleges and universities in satisfying society's needs.

Many students view colleges as a "reward" for hard work in high school. But the real role of universities is to meet the educational needs of the society. That's why universities receive tax exemptions. You got into college because you were motivated and society understands that it's better off with more black lawyers and doctors and leaders.

Moreover, a direct reason why black communities don't have the human resources they need is because for a long time they were denied access to education. However, if you receive a preference because the larger community needs educated citizens, you also incur a responsibility. Brandon Balthazer, a management consultant, reminds black students that "You don't have to justify yourself to anyone else, but you are obligated to do more than simply looking out for yourself."

Celebrate the Black heritage in higher education.

Learn about your black alumni. Fath Davis Ruffins points out that historically black colleges weren't the only source of black leaders. "At Harvard alone," she comments, "giving black students there a chance produced W.E.B. Dubois, Charles Hamilton Houston, Alain Locke, Ralph Bunche, and others."

Teach other students how our struggle has benefitted them.

For example, black colleges were havens for Holocaust survivors after WWII, and for Jewish scholars during the McCarthy period. The civil rights movement did much to silence conservatives who argued that women were taking spaces from "more qualified" men. And, without the student aid bills championed by black congressmen Adam Clayton Powell and Gus Hawkins, many working class white students today could never afford higher education.

Take a stand on principles that will support you in the long run.

You can never win by advocating censorship, or being racist or anti-Semitic or sexist. Peter Ivan Armstrong, also an administrative fellow, declares, "We can not be selectively tolerant. As a black southerner I do consider the Confederate flag a symbol of racism and violence. But when a white student hung a Confederate flag out of her window, I supported the university president's decision to allow her to do it."

You don't, however, have to passively accept racist behavior. Campuses value civility and eloquence. "If someone can only engage in free speech by calling you a nasty name," Armstrong muses, "you should insist that anyone who calls themselves college students should be more articulate."

Adopt an international perspective.

Many colleges offer a chance to spend some time abroad. If you get the opportunity, take it. There are few things that can give you a better perspective on being black in America than spending several months overseas.

133

Even if you can't actually travel to another country, go out of your way to meet foreign students. It can be eye-opening to discover how being black in the USA is both the same — and very different — than being black in Europe, Africa, or South America.

Take advantage of black studies courses.

Unfortunately, some black student avoid taking courses in black studies because they think that being black automatically makes them experts on the black experience, or are afraid that other people won't take these courses seriously. This is a terrible mistake. Studying black history and culture can really enrich your life and help you cope with stress. For example, many black intellectuals have spent a lot of time pondering how to maintain a healthy black identity without cutting themselves off from the experiences and resources available in the wider society.

Don't let anyone tell you who your friends should be.

Black students often come under enormous peer pressure concerning their friends. If you date someone who is not black, your friends accuse you of "going out with the enemy." If you only have black friends, people (both black and white) accuse you of segregating yourself. But the bottom line is that you have the right to be friends with anyone you choose, Period. "I don't care what anyone thinks," notes Cecile Scoon, an attorney, "You just don't have to make an either/or choice of friends."

Don't hesitate to ask for help if you need it.

When they're having problems coping with school, many students (black and white) don't take adequate advantage of the help that is available until it's too late. Don't wait till you're failing, or feeling seriously depressed. Speak to an advisor while there's still some time to drop a course, get some tutoring, or take an incomplete.

Most black faculty members, administrators, and sometimes even graduate students, feel that part of their role is to be available to the black students on campus. Former high school teachers can be a good source of advice. If the campus counseling service makes you uncomfortable, seek help off campus.

Don't give up on good grades.

Freshman year, many students have an adjustment period during which they don't do particularly well. Most colleges and universities understand this. The biggest problem with this slump is that it can convince you that you'll never be an honors student, so you don't try to make dean's list sophomore year, when you could probably do much better.

Don't give up on improving your transcript. One way to pull up a mediocre GPA is to take extra courses during the summer. A string of just three or four "A"s can give a graduate school, or employer, a favorable impression of your ability to work and persevere.

Save your indignation for truly important confrontations.

Roberta Morton, now a legal defense lawyer, suggests, "Do your best, don't let racism distract you, and don't come expecting a problem."

Don't forget why you're in school.

It's not primarily to change things or to have a great time. It's to take advantage of the college's resources in order to get an educational experience that will benefit you and your community.

Paul Ruffins '76, is a journalist with an MA degree in psychological counseling. Fath Davis Ruffins, '76, a historian, was president of Afro, Harvard's black student organization in the 70s. An earlier version of this essay first appeared in the Washington Post.

35. LATINO AND HISPANIC STUDENTS

A strong family life, a sense of solidarity with the community, and a deep commitment to a faith are great sources of satisfaction. What Latino and Hispanic students have to watch out for is that these strengths do not become obstacles to their success in the classroom. An overemphasis on family obligations has hurt many a college career.

Hispanic and Latino women are under heavy pressure to be selfless. Their lack of a strong sense of self-interest, studies show, accounts for their doing worse in school than men of their cultures. A relative in Puerto Rico dies and a young woman will immediately fly to the island without a word of explanation to her professors. An aunt gets sick in El Paso and her niece will leave college in Fort Worth to take care of her.

Latino and Hispanic students need to put themselves and future careers first, according to Alfred Castaneda, in *The Educational Needs of Minority Groups*. He, and other experts, are not recommending you become callous or give up what makes your heritage special. What they suggest is that you develop a perspective which emphasizes the importance of college in your life.

Only a profound emergency, one in which your intervention will make a *real* difference, is an acceptable excuse to abandon your studies. This means not being distracted by everything that comes along. What has to count for you is planning ahead. Constantly keep the connection clear in your mind between college and a better future.

It's all too easy to justify slipping away, because so few Hispanics or Latinos teach in or administer colleges and universities. School officials become a distant "them" in charge of everything. Thinking this way makes you feel powerless. When you make any positive contact with professors and administrators, whatever their linguistic backgrounds, you feel a part of an institution in which you are making an emotional investment.

Building these vital personal connections with figures in authority requires overcoming early training. Hispanic and Latino families insist their children give *respecto* to elders. A mother will make it clear to her child that it's improper to address remarks to a teacher, unless questioned or spoken to first. Children are told not to look the teacher in the eye. The Anglo teacher, not understanding this background, thinks these students are uninterested, because they never initiate a discussion, and disrespectful, because they look away when they are addressed.

You can't count on your professors to figure this out on their own. To succeed, according to experts, you have to change. Breaking away from any early training which holds you back in a predominantly Anglo institution won't be easy. Any time you reject an aspect of your culture to fit in, it is painful.

Statistics show that Latinos or Hispanics delay selecting majors. Career guidance will help you make a direct connection between your major and the job you want.

Regarding course work, be cautious in which Spanish language classes you enroll. Often it will be an unpleasant experience to take an ordinary beginning course, which you naturally expect to breeze through, only to discover the teacher insists upon structured grammar and the supremacy of Castilian Spanish, attacking certain variants as inferior or corrupted. This is a nasty business you can do little about. Look, instead, for courses with titles like "Spanish for Native Speakers."

135

Be realistic about setting a timetable for graduating. So what if your community college schedules the AA to take four semesters. Over 20% of Latinos and Hispanics who get this degree put in ten semesters, but they get it. The same slow, but steady, rate is found in senior colleges. The important thing is to keep coming back, term after term, until you finish.

Your parents can be a huge help to you if they have a positive attitude towards your schooling. Experience may have led them to be indifferent to the value of formal learning, or to have feelings of futility about the predominantly Anglo educational system. If so, work with them to help them to see the value of education that is so clear to you.

TAKING ON ACTIVISM

Self-interest is not enough for every student. Almost 60% of all undergrads believe that an individual can still change society, according to the most recent study by the Carnegie Foundation. There are plenty of kids coming out of high school, hoping to find that political activism for positive change is still a part of campus life. These, usually very bright, students become depressed upon discovering that the only "action" on their campuses is in the social life. They still see things that need to be changed, no matter how sheep-like they find their classmates. There are few organizations on campus designed to help out. If you want to do it, you will have to do it on your own, with a few friends.

Student activists traditionally take up liberal or left-wing causes. These have included peace, civil rights, environment, and civil liberties. College students are effecting enormous changes in the American response to apartheid, as they force many universities to sell stock issued by companies which do business in South Africa. The Ralph Nader-inspired public interest research groups (PIRG) recruit students to go into the community to lobby on environmental and other issues.

A similar, if smaller, development has been the rise of student involvement in conservative and right-wing concerns. The big movement here, which any student so inclined can hook into, is the "family issue" and a return to what are thought by some as "traditional" values. Supporting anti-communist groups around the world is another rallying point.

A major aspect of activism is organizing for and supporting political candidates. Students on the right or the left who choose to be activists get themselves noticed.

Eddie was a one-man band of opinions. He would slouch around in his old Army jacket, digging up figures on administration slush funds. He pushed sluggish student politicos into a frenzy by raising issues at public meetings, and by protesting the packing of insignificant committees. He had no mandate to expose indiscretions, because he wasn't on the newspaper staff or serving in any official capacity. It was just that he had a keen sense of raising a ruckus. On an isolated campus students have to create their own action. If not for him, the student newspaper would have had no lead story each week except "Dean Announces New Athletic Policy" or "Spring Pep Rally Poorly Attended."

When Eddie found a national policy with which he disagreed, he would beg for money from students and faculty so that he could buy ad space in the community newspaper. By the time he graduated, with honors, he had the admiration of some, and the respect of many. He also had had as exciting a college career as anyone could ask for.

One bonus for college activists is that they learn lessons which last a lifetime. The best kind of self-education is to look upon the world into which we were born with some healthy skepticism. Activists stand up for themselves or for the rights of those dear to them. Pity the school board that is arbitrary when dealing with an ex-activist's child, or the company that pollutes their neighborhood.

36. MAKING EXCITEMENT: INTELLECTUAL LIFE

"Dull," "blah," "beat" — that's how a vast number of students describe their campuses. Only the party scene and athletics bring out any enthusiasm. There is little political activism around, and the classes people take to prepare for professional careers don't offer much excitement. After their first term, students start feeling vaguely cheated, without knowing why. Students say they wish they could recapture the once widespread sense that college was the single most interesting place to be in the whole society.

Who's to blame? Not students, because they're just responding to signals from bosses, parents, legislators, and deans. "They" lay out the course of instruction, and subtly direct the choices you make. Following their agenda is painfully boring.

There are just too many intensely uninteresting, repetitious courses out there now. You have to break through this deadening round of plodding, head-down classwork, because boredom leads to fatigue, which cuts down on your efficiency. A high percentage of the students who drop out do so because they can't find anything interesting to hold them to their work schedules.

So what if the intellectual and political climate on your campus is slack? If you can make ideas count for you, personally, the college experience comes alive. Here's a closely guarded secret: there is one group on every campus which lives for ideas — the professors. Some of them are quite interesting and friendly. An astonishing number enjoy talking intense-ly with students. Developing a social life that includes your profs helps you mature faster than if you spend all your spare time hanging out with friends your own age.

Permit yourself to take classes in departments far different from your major, to plug into fresh intellectual excitement. The issues and questions raised by philosophy, English, history, political science, biology, religion, psychology or sociology will stimulate you.

This is not just a pitch for the liberal arts or social sciences. There are plenty of interesting, non-technical courses in the natural and physical sciences, in theater, music, and the arts. Departments with low enrollments are the places to get intimate seminars with teachers who make an extra effort.

Finding exciting, off-beat courses is only the start. Having the right attitude towards how to learn is far more important. You create intellectual excitement by being willing to wrestle with tough material, track down definitions on your own, and generate questions about what interests you. Don't be thrown by initial confusion and uncertainty. If the light doesn't break, check out more books or try another experiment. The big reward is the flash of enlightenment when it hits.

Everything is *not* known. There is an enormous amount yet to be discovered in every field. "It is important that students bring a certain rag muffin barefoot irreverence to their studies," Jacob Bronowski, a scientist, insists: "They are not here to worship what is known, but to question it."

137

CRIB NOTES ON COLLEGE NOVELS

Authors who went to college write novels about the subject. This makes sense, when you think about it.

Love Story by Erich Segal — In the author's own words: "a very short novel about a Harvard boy, old New England, and a Radcliffe girl, Italian-American, who fall in love...and then are struck by tragedy." In the movie, Ali McGraw gets "Hollywood disease," whereby an actress gets better and better looking in her hospital bed until she passes away from terminal beauty.

Giles Goat Boy: Or, The Revised New Syllabus by John Barth — This book is huge: 710 pages of allegorical density. The university as Universe. The Hero (Billy Bocksfuss) as a boy raised to be a goat on an experimental farm. The Reader as...well, figure it out for yourself. This one may show up on your assigned reading list, so get ready.

The War Between the Tates by Alison Lurie — A novel centering on a faculty family at Corinth (read: Cornell) University. A marriage breaks apart and comes together again. Bickering, sharp dialogue, petty academic squabbling, and adultery made for a best seller.

This Side of Paradise by F. Scott Fitzgerald — How it was to be young, rich, good looking, and amoral at Princeton in the Twenties. This first novel deals with the adventures of Amory Blaine, probably a great guy to have in your club — but you wouldn't introduce him to your sister.

The Paper Chase by John Jay Osburn, Jr. — Stress, stress, and still more stress in the first year of law school. Why anyone who took Contract Law with a cold fish like Professor Kingsfield would worship him as a hero is a tough one to figure. But then again, there are people who admire G. Gordon Liddy.

Breaking Away by Joseph Howard — The movie puts the bicycle riding up front. The novel concentrates more heavily on tensions between the locals ("cutters") and the students, especially fraternity members. Our hero has it both ways in the town-gown conflict, eventually enrolling in college yet keeping his old friends.

The 158 Pound Marriage by John Irving — An early novel by the author of *The World According to Garp*. Departmental wife-swapping combined with college wrestling. The tag-teams are a history professor with wife and wrestling coach with spouse. Irving does a better job describing the matches on the mat than the mismatches in bed.

Lucky Jim by Kingsley Amis — The uproarious adventures of a young Don Quixote who drifts through English university life, questing after a teaching job. Best scene — when he attempts to deliver a vital lecture while totally snookered. As soon as he drops his delusion that he belongs in academe he lands a good job and meets a fine woman.

37. YOUR TRACK

To some students, a semi-formal outfit means putting on jeans, rather than sweats. Others won't walk out the door without an hour's preparation to achieve a perfectly coordinated outfit. There's no one way to dress for every campus, and the same diversity goes for social and academic life.

Certain students are "all work and no play" types who fall into a driven style, which reduces their social contacts to a minimum. There may have been early family pressure on them, or else they come from a cultural tradition that puts the premium upon heavy study time and intense specialization. Another group of students fall into this same category because they pitch themselves into preparation for extremely demanding majors. Any socializing comes at rare slack moments, and is a bonus.

Other students concentrate upon development of an aggressive social life. They take up hectic, not to say frantic, socializing because that's what they learned to value from their family and community. "Not much school and lots of play" characterizes the pattern of getting into a deepening round of parties, organizations, and sports. On a campus with a party reputation, these students are tempted to bury their classwork under an avalanche of extracurricular activities and plenty of drinking.

The ancient Greeks advised moderation in all things. Still a useful notion. Individuals who make studies the only focus of their lives are in danger of burning out, and of leaving school unprepared to deal with the social complexities of the non-academic world. The folks who carefully avoid the library sometimes get excellent grades, but it's more likely they will get into trouble with their classes.

Experts point out that the majority of successful students follow a standard pattern. These students are rarely aware that they're all taking the same road. It's time to bring this unobserved pattern out into the open. What you do with the information is up to you.

This standard pattern resembles the good old grading bell curve. In their first semester, students who are going to survive find some friends, get out and experience as much as possible, and push through their introductory courses. Within a year or so they make enough friends, figure out what they most like to do with their time, and find classwork to be manageable. In the last few semesters random socializing falls off, but successful students never become hermits. If you are having trouble in school, or in your social life, imitate this proven pattern, and see if it helps.

GLOSSARY OF COLLEGESPEAK

AA: The A.A. (Associate of Arts) and the A.S. (Associate of Science) are the two most common degrees issued by community colleges. They traditionally take four semesters to complete.

ACADEMIC: Having to do with college and university life. (Looks back to the ancient Greek philosopher, Plato, who founded a school named the Academy.) Variations: *academia, academe*.

ACADEMIC YEAR: Runs from late August/early September to the end of June/beginning of July.

ACT (AMERICAN COLLEGE TEST): One of two major college entrance examinations. The other is the SAT.

ADVANCED PLACEMENT: The admission of a freshman to an advanced course in college, based upon an exam given in high school.

AFFIRMATIVE ACTION: The steps taken by a university or employer to guarantee nondiscrimination against minorities and women.

ALUMNUS: Latin for a male graduate of a college, university or institution of learning. (Plural is *alumni*.) The feminine is *alumna* (plural is *alumnae*).

BA, BS (BACHELOR OF ARTS AND BACHELOR OF SCIENCE): The two principal degrees granted to undergraduates who have successfully completed a program which traditionally takes four years.

BLUE BOOKS: Lined paper booklets for essay exams provided by professors. Some schools sell them at bookstores.

BURSAR (TREASURER, OR COMPTROLLER): The official in charge of the financial and business affairs of a university or college.

CAMPUS: The grounds and structures of a college or university. Sometimes called the "quad" or "yard." In broadest use, refers to the institution itself.

CATALOG (UNIVERSITY BULLETIN, COLLEGE PROGRAM): A bound booklet setting out the course of study at a college or university, along with the institution's procedures and policies.

CHAIRPERSON (CHAIR, CHAIRMAN, HEAD OF DEPARTMENT): Faculty member, of any rank, elected by his or her fellow teachers (or appointed by the administration) to direct a department.

CLEP (COLLEGE LEVEL EXAMINATION PROGRAM): A test administered by the College Board that determines the eligibility for college credit of non-traditional or life learning experiences.

CONCENTRATION: Course of study in a department followed by a non-major. Needs fewer departmental course points and requirements than a major.

CO-OP: Cooperative organization set up and run by students to sell books, records, food, or other items at reduced prices.

COURSE OFFERING BULLETIN (OR SCHEDULE OF CLASSES): A listing of classes for each semester or term. Includes day, time, location, credit hours and instructor.

CRAMMING: Intensive preparation for an examination, usually the night before.

CREDIT: The point value used as the unit of academic measurement. Each course carries a point value based upon its degree of difficulty or the number of hours it meets per week.

CURRICULUM: The program of study — or the courses — offered by a college or a university.

DEAN: Administrative official who reports to the president or vice president about the running of academic divisions (liberal arts, natural sciences, etc.), or upon various aspects of student life.

DEAN'S LIST: Honor roll each term (or marking period) for students who meet the GPA standards set by each college or university.

DEFERRED ADMISSION: The program some colleges and universities have of allowing new students to hold off entering college for a short or long period after acceptance.

DEPARTMENT: Self-governing unit of scholars and creative people. Consists of faculty, chairperson, secretaries, and TAs.

DOCTOR: Title for person who has been awarded the Ph.D. (Doctor of Philosophy), Ed.D (Doctor of Education), J.D. (Juris Doctor). A teacher may be a "professor" without this degree.

DRAFT (OF A PAPER): First, or preliminary, form of any writing, which will be revised or copied.

EMERITUS: A professor who is retired from service with special distinction.

ESSAY: A composition on a particular subject. Used to describe both a required paper or an answer to an examination question.

EXTRACURRICULAR ACTIVITIES: College and university life beyond what goes on in the classroom. Includes student government, clubs, teams, and other non-academic organizations.

FACULTY ADVISOR: A professor or staff member assigned to assist students in making up their programs and to answer their questions. Some schools require a student to visit an advisor prior to registration, while other schools make the visit optional.

FEES: Charges assessed by a college or university for attending which cover tuition, housing, food plan, student activities, medical insurance, and other non-tuition items.

GMAT (GRADUATE MANAGEMENT APTITUDE TEST): Generally required for admission to an MBA program at a grad business school. Administered by the same people who write the SATs.

GPA (GRADE POINT AVERAGE): An assessment of a student's overall performance. It is the average of all grades, weighed by the number of semester (or trimester or quarter) units each course is worth.

GRE (GRADUATE RECORD EXAMINATION): An exam administered to candidates for graduate school by the same people who write the SATs.

GUT: Slang name for a popular course presumed to be extremely easy.

HUMANITIES: The academic disciplines of literature, philosophy, languages, music, fine arts, history, theater, and religion. More of an academic subdivision of knowledge than a field of study in itself.

INDEPENDENT STUDY: Supervised individual work on a special topic, usually designed by the student. The department has to approve the project and a faculty member must agree to supervise the work.

INTERLIBRARY LOAN: The lending of library materials from one college or university to another.

INTERNSHIP: On-the-job, field experience for which the student may gain college credit.

INTRAMURAL SPORTS: Team or individual play within and among the student body.

IVY LEAGUE: An association (originally set up as an athletic conference) of prestigious Eastern universities — Brown, Columbia, Cornell, Dartmouth, Harvard, University of Pennsylvania, Princeton, and Yale. The term "Ivy League" has come to stand for elitism and prestige.

141

LAB SECTION: Laboratory session attached to a course, typically for additional point credit.

LEARNING LAB: Service offered by some colleges and universities for improvement of skills in writing, mathematics, and peer tutoring in a variety of fields.

LIBERAL ARTS: A traditional program of study which provides a general knowledge of the world and develops intellectual capacities, rather than offering a scientific, technical, professional, or vocational education.

LSAT (LAW SCHOOL ADMISSION TEST): Generally required for admission to law school. Administered by the same people who write the SATs.

MAJOR: Can stand for both the person who majors and the subject itself. Involves upper division study in one department, following an established sequence of courses and the fulfilling of various requirements.

MATRICULATION: The formal admission to full membership and privileges for a registered student who has met the requirements set by the college or university. A student who has not matriculated will often be allowed to take courses, but will not receive a degree until the qualifications are fulfilled.

MCAT (MEDICAL COLLEGE ADMISSION TEST): Generally required for admission to medical school. Administered by the same people who write the SATs.

MENTOR: Informally, refers to any older person who assists and guides a younger person. In non-traditional colleges and universities, refers to a faculty member assigned to supervise independent work.

PARAPHRASE: To rewrite in one's own words, keeping to the intention and sense of the original, giving credit to the original to avoid plagiarism.

PASS/FAIL OPTION: A student may elect this option as an alternative to a letter grade. (Usually is not permitted in the major or concentration.) Typically, the professor is not notified who has requested this option, so the final grade is set by the registrar.

PEER COUNSELOR: An experienced student who helps other students cope with college-related academic and social problems.

PLAGIARISM: To copy another's words or ideas and present them as one's own, without giving credit to the originator.

PREP SCHOOL: Preparatory school. An expensive private high school intended to prepare a self-selected elite for college.

PREREQUISITES: The early courses in a sequence. May be a general survey in advance of specialized courses, lower-division courses before upper-division courses, or any necessary preparation for a field.

PROBATION: Notification to students that their progress towards a degree is unsatisfactory, due to low grades or disciplinary violations. If grades or conduct do not improve, students may be suspended or required to withdraw.

PROVOST: The chief university administrator under the president in charge of academic or educational activities.

RA (RESIDENT ASSISTANT): A Resident Counselor in a dormitory. At larger institutions this position may be held by a grad student or an employee.

REGISTRAR: An officer who maintains the records of students.

RESUME: A brief summing up on paper of experience in work, school, and extracurricular activities for the purpose of gaining employment.

ROTC (RESERVE OFFICERS' TRAINING CORPS): An on-campus program to provide college-trained officers for the armed forces.

SABBATICAL: Paid leave of absence granted to a professor to undertake a creative project.

SAT (SCHOLASTIC APTITUDE TEST): Multiple-choice exam, administered by the College Entrance Examination Board. Used by colleges and universities to evaluate applicants.

SEMESTER: See TERM.

SEMINAR: Small class where students are expected to participate actively and sometimes to discuss the results of their research.

SYLLABUS: An outline of the term's work prepared by an instructor listing readings, due dates for exams and papers, special requirements, and (sometimes) supplemental readings. Has the unofficial nature of an implied agreement between the instructor and the student.

TA (TEACHING ASSISTANT): A paid, or unpaid, graduate student who teaches sections under a professor's direction, grades papers, or undertakes other scholarly duties for the department in which he or she is taking advanced work.

TENURE: A permanent position granted a professor after a probationary period. The faculty member is thereafter assured employment, unless misconduct or incompetence is proven.

TERM: A division of the academic year, as in a semester, trimester, or quarter.

THESIS: An author's interpretation of the material under consideration. Not to be confused with what the reading concerns (subject) or the data (evidence) used to back up the author's point(s). Also the name of the written project sometime required to receive advanced degrees.

TOEFL EXAM (TEST OF ENGLISH AS A FOREIGN LANGUAGE): An examination often required of foreign students before they will be admitted to an American university.

TRANSCRIPT: Cumulative list issued to students by the registrar's office every term showing courses taken and grades awarded. This is the official record of a student's academic activities.

TUITION: The money required to enroll for a course of study. Does not include fees.

UNDERGRADUATE: A matriculated student, following a course of study, who has not yet received a bachelor's degree.

UNIVERSITY: An institution of higher education that has an undergraduate college and at least one graduate school (medicine, law, engineering, etc.).

VARSITY SPORTS: Sanctioned sports teams organized to play the teams of other schools. A student who officially makes the team receives a "varsity letter," which is the initial of the school's name.

WORK-STUDY PROGRAM: The College Work-Study Program is an employment plan for students in need of financial assistance, financed by the federal government. It includes part-time jobs during the academic year and full-time jobs during the summer.

ACKNOWLEDGMENTS

The authors would like to thank the following individuals for their help, advice, and encouragement in writing this book. (Institutional affiliations are only for the purpose of identification.)

Art Budington, Nichols School
Lewis Cobury, State University of New York at Buffalo
Elwin Powell, State University of New York at Buffalo
Michael Cummings, Roswell Park Institute
Joy Kassett, National Institute of Mental Health
Carol Frank, Erie County Community College
Jerry Evans, Erie County Community College
Nancy Bowser, Fredonia College
William Clark, Fredonia College
Robert Coon, Fredonia College
Michael Dimitri, Fredonia College
James Hurtgen, Fredonia College
Kathy Lugo / Olga Mandel
Alice Rosenthal / Margarite Kelly
Gail McCarthy, Niagara County Community College
Elana Lozan Vranich, College of St. Elizabeth
Nicholas Cushner, Empire State College
Thomas Rocco, Empire State College

Students from Columbia College, Fredonia College, and Niagara County Community College who read the manuscript along the way and offered insightful criticism include Sarah Morgentha, Joel Goldberg, Tom Webb, Betsy Buzack, Tina Spinelli, Darren Martin, and Maureen Salter.

Our special thanks to Mary Notaro, who typed the first drafts, and, especially, to Joanne Foeller, who carefully read the material while putting it into a form suitable for publication.

The jacket photograph was taken by Denise Wood.

Layout and illustrations are by Casey Smith and Beth Fabiano.